# 'Life's Bi

## "You Are Not Who You Think You Are"

### By Rany Athwall

Copyright 2019 Rany Athwall – All Rights Reserved

ISBN: 978-0-244-81781-7

# Table of Contents

**Introduction**

## Part 1

|  |  |  |
|---|---|---|
|  | My First Experience | 9 |
| Chapter One: | The Mental Beginning | 15 |
| Chapter Two: | Life's Early Conditioning | 22 |
| Chapter Three: | Identifying Needs | 35 |
| Chapter Four: | Down Memory Lane | 47 |
| Chapter Five: | It's Just a Thought | 55 |
| Chapter Six: | Emotional Impact | 62 |
| Chapter Seven: | What's Your Role? | 70 |
| Chapter Eight: | The Complete Project | 79 |
| Chapter Nine: | Life's Big Questions | 85 |
| Chapter Ten: | Is This the End? | 92 |

# Table of Contents

## Part 2

| | | |
|---|---|---|
| Chapter Eleven: | Let's Reflect | 98 |
| Chapter Twelve: | Your True Self | 108 |
| Chapter Thirteen: | Become the Silent Witness | 117 |
| Chapter Fourteen: | Humanity Is One | 126 |
| Chapter Fifteen: | Let Emotions Flow | 137 |
| Chapter Sixteen: | Allow Life to Happen | 145 |
| Chapter Seventeen: | Stop Limiting Your Greatness | 153 |
| Chapter Eighteen: | Your Natural State | 160 |
| Chapter Nineteen: | Simply Amazing | 170 |
| Chapter Twenty: | Being Thoughtless | 177 |
| Chapter Twenty-One: | Finally Free | 184 |

## About the Author

Rany Athwall is an author, mind mentor and coach who is committed to improving the lives of people who are struggling with their mental health and any other aspect of their lives. His profound understanding and personal experience of the mind can help humans to get in touch with their true self and reach levels they never knew existed.

Life's Biggest Con is a thought provoking and engaging guide to understanding and recognising your real-self. He describes how the created-self developed throughout life, from birth to school days and into adulthood, in a way which many people will relate to.

# Thank You

As I began to start this writing book, I realised the complexity of trying to share my realisation in words. I knew how simple my message was, but equally putting it into words without confusing the reader wasn't going to be a simple task. However, I decided irrespective of the challenge, that even if it helped one person to have a better life, then my effort would be rewarded.

To my wonderful wife Daya, and two amazing children Mya & Raul. Without their encouragement and support, I wouldn't have found the time or inspiration to write this book. Thank you!

# Introduction

Why do so many people find life burdensome? Why do humans suffer on a daily basis, worrying about the future, struggling with their relationships, careers, finances, and health? Worse yet, because of their mindset, many suffer regularly from anxiety, depression, and many other types of negative mental states and illnesses, making life a living hell. Rather than living, humans have become frightened of what they have created with their minds and search for some relief. Humans have become accustomed to many habits and behaviors that are destroying and making their lives worse instead of better. Even some of the lesser destructive habits humans adopt are picked up in the hope of any respite and break they can find from themselves. In essence, humans have become their own worst enemy, scared of life and their minds. It is a sad reality of the modern world that mental health issues, poor decisions, and constant conflict are what we humans are fighting against every day, and it is getting worse all the time. To see a change, we must first accept that we are ultimately responsible for what we have unintentionally created with our minds. Only then can we begin to make a difference to this everyday mediocre existence and negative mental state.

So what have you been creating with your mind, and who are you? We are all unique, and the answer to the above question will undoubtedly come in many forms and descriptions. Many factors have influenced what you believe about yourself: your family, your upbringing, the education you received, the skills you have acquired, your relationships, your financial situation, and your religious beliefs. All of these experiences accumulated together is who you believe you are today; however, by the end of reading this book, you will discover this is not who you are. Some of you may not be ready to understand this or even want or need to know, but for everyone else, it will change everything; the way you think, the way you behave, how you feel about your past, the present, and your future. I haven't written about any miracles or about any concepts, about religion or any external power that is going to intervene and change your life forever. Instead, I'm going to give you an insight from my personal experience that you are much more than what you think and believe about yourself. If you want to live a life of happiness and one without worry, change the way you view problems, remove the fear that uncertainty brings, and embrace every day with passion. There is only one place to start. You must begin to realize that you are not who you think you are.

But before I do that, I want to start by sharing with you why I wrote this book. Over time, I have experienced and discovered an awareness of the real me. This feeling has been with me as far back as I can remember, however, its true meaning and understanding has been a process and only developed over time. I now experience this part of me daily, and this has changed my perception of everything about who I am and about my life. I now want to share this awareness with you, and once you fully understand, you too will begin to notice your life changing for the better. It will bring about an understanding that will transform your life and the lives of others around you; it will change how you view anything you have a thought about, and it removes anything and everything you aren't happy or feeling good about. You will, for the first time, experience life without fear and every day will be a fantastic gift waiting for you to receive.

Also, in this book, I will go through some examples and experiences from my life, some of which I'm sure will resonate with you. I will also along the way be asking you some questions about your life to help you to understand more about who you think you are and why. I hope you don't mind because some of these questions might be personal. I will also illustrate my insight as to why humans are all being CONNED into believing who they are. Knowing the truth will improve anything about you and your life, your mental state, and how you deal with the pressures and stresses of life. It will improve your relationships, remove all limitations on what is possible for you, but above all else will bring true peace and fulfillment into your life.

This awareness will bring in a shift that I can only describe as profound and life-changing. I'm going to take you through a step-by-step process to win back your true self and start the course of losing the root cause of all your suffering and, for most parts, what's making your life difficult. There is a process to reading this book: for the truth to resonate correctly you must read it in the order the chapters are set out, and for better understanding, I have split the book into two parts. Part One is going to take you on a journey, whatever your age, to help you to understand your present state and how you became the person you believe you are today. It is imperative you know the various phases of how you've been using your mind throughout your life before you read Part Two. The second part of the book gives you an insight on how to get in touch with your true self and the difference this will make to your life.

# Quote

---

"In a gentle way, you can shake the world."
**-Mahatma Gandhi-**

---

# My First Experience

I was ten years old when I first experienced a strange and overwhelming feeling that I was more than what I thought. We used to live in a newly built estate in a small town called West Bromwich, in England, the UK, a quiet area. The estate was still relatively new, and it was considered the posh part of the town. I thoroughly enjoyed growing up there, and I have very fond memories of my childhood. The summer holidays were especially memorable. Playing out on the estate and the park nearby was terrific. The estate consisted of a few hundred houses, but wherever you were, you always felt comfortable in the surroundings because you knew everyone in some capacity.

In the summer months, for long hours of the day the sun would reflect onto the front door of our house. This one summer morning, the sun was somewhat stronger and brighter, and I opened the door and stood there for a while just sensing the heat against my face and body, looking into the street to see if anyone was outside playing who I could join. I was feeling alive at that moment and grateful for just being, and it was then, like a flash, that a sudden fear came over me with the thought that one day I would die and no longer exist. My heartbeat raced, and yet with all of the heat from the sun, I felt really cold and motionless for a couple of minutes. At the time, it felt like it was much longer, and when the feeling and thoughts subsided, I was left standing there in a state of confusion. Following the experience, I had an overwhelming feeling that I wasn't quite myself, and for the next few days, the experience and thoughts continued to trouble me. I was finding it difficult to focus; the idea of death terrified me, and even though in my mind it was potentially far away from happening, this realization had added another dimension to my existence.

A few months later, I started to develop very uncomfortable headaches and the standard painkillers weren't relieving the pain. I had no other symptoms, and the treatment from the doctor wasn't working either, so I was referred to the local hospital for further tests. During this time, my thoughts were undoubtedly making the headaches worse because I believed there was something seriously wrong with me. The test results didn't show anything, and the headaches were a complete mystery.

I was admitted to the children's ward at the hospital near my home for further examinations and for the doctors to monitor me more closely. A full week of X-rays, medication, round-the-clock care, and no nearer to finding out the cause or relieving the symptoms. One evening after visiting hours, I was lying in bed completely free of thought, and then suddenly the same fear of death struck me, only this time it lasted much longer and was backed up with an inner feeling of tranquility. The experience and thoughts about death occurred a few times while I was in the hospital, and it was beginning to scare me to the extent where I was having trouble eating and sleeping. I wanted to tell my family that I was scared of dying and that I was having these strange experiences, but I was too embarrassed to say anything. Besides this, it could quite easily have been a typical experience for someone who was in hospital fearing the worst. The headaches eventually stopped and I never really understood the cause. However, I now know that what happened that morning and while I was in the hospital was the beginning of what I would later discover about myself.

When I returned home from hospital, life quickly went back to normal; everything on the outside, that is, but internally, something felt different. I continued to have this feeling in brief moments throughout the following months; it was invariably a quick succession of intense fear followed by flashes of serenity and calmness. I lived in constant anticipation of them. These moments made me more conscious of my thoughts, and the experience became a part of my life. Over time, I became so comfortable with these thoughts that I didn't feel attached to them anymore. I experienced them, felt the emotions connected to them, but it was like I was just a witness looking in from the outside.

This feeling of duality became a regular experience growing up. It wasn't always clear, but in the background, I could detect a disparity with my thoughts. They switched from having a real connection and feeling towards them, to moments when I was merely watching them take place. Unfortunately, for someone so young, this was difficult to comprehend, and perhaps this was quite normal for a human being. I continued to have brief moments of duality with my thoughts until my early adult years when the feelings of duality weakened. On reflection, as a young adult, many of my decisions and lifestyle choices at that time offer a reasonable explanation as to why this could have happened. There were some conscious moments as an adult when I could briefly sense this feeling, but it was a fleeting experience and of no real value. As life took its inevitable path through time, I sorely missed the taste of duality, especially during moments that were challenging.

When I was young, I never fully recognized this unique understanding of thought and never appreciated its value or purpose. With age, my appreciation for what I had experienced developed and I tried many times in vain to initiate the thoughts that originated the duality in me, yet the harder I tried, the more elusive it became. Even during the periods of the frustration of wanting to rewind the clock and go back, there was still a background awareness. Unfortunately, I didn't have enough courage or willpower to make the changes that were needed. I had invested so much into the self and the lifestyle I so desired that giving it all up didn't seem worth it. Therefore, life as I knew it had to continue, while the predictable journey was in full flow. I never fully felt comfortable and what I knew and felt deep down was difficult to ignore. I had given in to the temptations of the world because it was the more natural thing to do.

However, I always knew there was more to understand about human existence and was convinced one day I would discover the truth about who I was. Many years later, I made a conscious decision to change many aspects of my life. I took a direction that I felt was needed. I had many unanswered questions regarding my life and its purpose. I made some tough decisions that completely changed the outlook of my life. Drastic alterations and sacrifices were made. It wasn't something I was comfortable with, and I suffered many moments of uncertainty. But I knew it was something I had to do without compromise and see it through to the end.

With perseverance, suddenly, I began to have very subtle glimpses of the duality I experienced when I was younger. It was over twenty-five years later, and at first, I was still in a state of uncertainty with many of my present thoughts and beliefs. Nonetheless, I remembered what that felt like, and it was a very poignant moment for me. The following years, I felt like I was in between two worlds and didn't belong to either. It was tough to grasp, and with so much doubt over my existence, left me feeling disordered and lost. I continued my journey of life with the hope that one day, I would experience something more, and the answer I needed would surface. Then when I least expected it, like a bolt of lightning, the day arrived that created an opening in me. It was the pivotal moment when I uncovered that what I wanted and feared were precisely the same. I had discovered the truth about human existence. It changed everything about me and my life in an instant. Words alone cannot describe this feeling and understanding. The peace, happiness, and serenity I feel is not something I could have ever imagined or experienced in the past.

I wanted to share this with the world but wasn't sure how until I had the idea of writing a book. For quite some time, I was undecided whether or not I would have the right words and techniques of explanation to share my realization with the world. I've always had the attitude that everyone deserves to be happier, to be more at peace with themselves and the world they live in. Therefore, I decided that irrespective of my abilities, I must make an effort to create the same opening in other humans, and to make a difference in their lives. So please sit back and enjoy the read, and however long it takes for you to read this book, you too will learn you are not who you think you are, and I will show you the way of being in touch with your true self.

# Quote

---

"If you're always trying to be normal, you will never know how amazing you can be."
**-Maya Angelou-**

---

# Chapter One:
# The Mental Beginning

I want to take you back to the day you were born, a non-thinking baby. I don't have an in-depth scientific explanation of what babies go through during the birthing process, but I'm sure when you were born, you didn't have an opinion or any thoughts of what had just happened or was happening to you. When you were a baby, you were at the beginning of the development process, which you later referred to as "me". As an infant, you were at the mercy of your parents and guardians to take care of you. The primary communication faculty you were born with was the ability to cry. Initially, the crying was used for feelings of discomfort, hunger, and any physical pain, so your parents and guardians could respond to your needs.

You are also born with an instinct for your survival. These are the reflexes of the body, movements of the eyes, mouth, neck, hands, and feet, which gave you the ability to respond. A few months into your life, you started recognizing people, you began responding to voices, your unconscious mind commenced the recording of your early experiences and your feelings towards them. You learned the necessary skills very quickly. You were extremely observant of what was happening around you, and you could absorb information very well. You started to identify with the environment you lived in, the various spaces and the people around you, even though there was still a lot of unconscious uncertainty. Your observation skills also expanded as you started to copy movements and sounds. Everything you saw, heard, and touched was an experience through your senses and from these experiences you began to distinguish what you were more comfortable with. This was followed by you discovering more about yourself, for example, the things you liked and disliked. Your imagination had grown, and you now had an understanding that you could get what you wanted by behaving a certain way.

The inner chatter had also started unconsciously to explain your feelings and thoughts about your experiences, even though your vocabulary was very limited. You also adopted some habits. You could define to some degree what made you happy and what made you sad. One advantage you had when you were young was that most of your needs to be happy were in the present moment since you didn't have too much of a past that could get in your way or any thoughts about a future. A tad older, needs were becoming a standard part of your daily life. It started with your parents and guardians understanding your needs, and soon after, using your imagination, you started thinking and creating needs for yourself. Do you remember the first time you created a need from thought and were conscious of it? This was when you realized your mind could piece together stories of what you would like to happen and it wasn't merely about needing something anymore, but it became more about imagining what was required on your part to fulfill a particular need. For this, you unconsciously learned to negotiate methods for your needs and how to get your way by using language and behavioral patterns you created from your limited life experience.

Although today, your first few years as an infant and child won't feel of any real significance, these early years shouldn't be underestimated as to the influence they had on your thoughts. It was a critical time of your development, and it was the foundation of how you would react to situations and interpret experiences in the next few years of life. The early emotions were extremely significant; mental pain and pleasure helped you to make choices in your life. Fear always takes the pedestal of your emotions. Even very early on, much of what you considered for your development was to avoid experiencing any fear, and conversely, anything you experienced to be pleasurable you would want to repeat more often. As a child, you were either playing or learning. Most of the time you enjoyed the playing part more than the learning, although this isn't the case for everyone. This is the all-too-familiar pattern later in life too. This initial conditioning set you up for the forthcoming phase of your life, especially the educational years. You are not likely to remember much at all from those early years; in fact, you may only recall a small segment of information about your life as a child. However, with everything that you went through, your mind was unconsciously recording and presenting information as and when it was called upon in the years to come.

Through my early years, I don't remember too much about myself, other than stories my parents and family have told me over the years, for example, the type of things I used to do as a child and about many of my habits. But I've often thought what if most of this was made up or even exaggerated because I don't remember much and even if I did, it's very vague. I also noticed growing up that some of the stories my parents told about me changed over the years from their perspective and memory of what happened. Even though I don't remember experiencing any of them, I do hold mental images and thoughts about what I was told. Some of these events are probably irrelevant, but what is essential to understand is how easily humans can identify with a past that is made up of stories that aren't true. There may also be experiences from your childhood that you have deliberately exaggerated to make yourself appear more interesting to others, and eventually you started to believe this too. The human mind is known to do this under many circumstances. All mental images and thoughts become ingrained in our minds for future reference and become a part of our life's conditioning, whether they are true or not, especially those we have attached strong emotions to. During your life, so much changes in your mind about your past because of the various mental states you go through, and you can never be entirely sure about anything. Even some of the authentic experiences could be construed as inaccurate and open to question by your mind.

My first understanding of the tricks our minds play was from my preschool days. Often, I would see other children either being shouted at or being punished by the teachers for behaving badly. The outcome would be them getting upset or feeling humiliated in front of the class. By observing their experience and having a mental image in my mind, the experience would feel like my own. This is how the mind works; each experience, whether it is yours or imagined, becomes part of your mind's recorded data and conditioning. Even at such a young age, our imagination starts creating our reality, not from something that has happened but from thought. This continues to take place throughout our lives, expressing the nature of how our mind can deceive us and make us believe anything. You may ask, "Why is this important?" and "What difference does this make to my life today?" if what you remember about your past isn't all true, especially if it isn't affecting how you feel now. And you are absolutely right, but what is important to understand is how humans believe their past is who they are, yet you can still believe in whatever you want today about your past.

Consciously and unconsciously, your mind changes and adjusts your thoughts depending on how you want to feel and what you want to believe about yourself, whether it is true or not. The mental story of who you are had truly started.

# Remember

You were born as a non-thinking baby

---

You were at the beginning of the development process

---

You began to discern between what made you happy and sad

---

You had an understanding that you could get what you wanted by behaving a certain way

---

The mental story of who you are had truly started

# Quote

_____

"Nothing is good or bad, thinking makes it so."
**-William Shakespeare-**

_____

# Chapter Two:
# Life's Early Conditioning

When we consider the development of a child or even a young adult, we are referring to the physical and mental development. Physical development relates to physical attributes, whereas mental development refers to the character traits that are a combined result of education and early life experience. Humans in Western society go through several educational stages in their lives, starting with infancy, preschool, primary levels, and going on to secondary school and, in some cases, even university. Learning is something you continue to do in your life whatever your age or phase. Nevertheless, the years between infancy and the teenage years are the most fundamental to the development of who you become and what you believe about yourself today.

Without using too many psychology ideals and methods, let's look briefly into the effects your environment and people had on you in those early years. In this next phase of your life, you developed more of an awareness of your environment, where you lived and its surroundings. In your mind it became your very own miniature world that you shared with the people in your life. In this space, you felt secure and comfortable; it was your territory, you took ownership over that personal space, and you determined how you would behave in those confinements. The only rules you had to abide by were from your parents and guardians. This setting hugely influenced your early upbringing. This was the place where you were more confident and assured about yourself. You were very protective over this space, and people from the outside weren't always welcome. Conversely, outside of your home, it was a very different story, one of not being so confident and secure. This is when most children experience fear properly for the first time, by being exposed to something new. There is nothing unusual about experiencing the insecurity away from what you know and are comfortable with; this is all part of the human programming. It takes time for the mind to adjust to new surroundings and especially change.

During this time, you also became more obsessive towards loved ones and certain individuals. Your attachment to them strengthened, as did your expectations of them. Your unconscious understanding and belief were that a personal commitment to protect you from harm had been agreed, and this made you feel dependent on them. These are the very people you turned to for your emotional needs. Similarly, they are the first group of people that gave you a sense of belonging and understanding of trust. Furthermore, in their presence, you started to observe their behavior more strictly by creating and recording mental images of their actions. You played mental games by imitating them and acting out their roles.

However, most of the habits you adopted from your parents and siblings were unconscious. It included their reactions, their choice of language, and some of their more noticeable emotions. It is very natural and intuitive for children to copy and imitate the people they occupy the most time with. Your first home and the people you were exposed to in those early years had a strong influence on who you would become later in life, particularly how you understood the environment around you and what was considered as normal behavior. For instance, some children grow up in an environment where shouting at each other is a common everyday experience, whereas for others, just raising your voice is not accepted. So you can begin to understand how many of your habits today are a direct result of what you recorded mentally from your experiences as a child with your family.

As you progressed, you started to establish an opinion about the people in your life. You would single out anyone you felt more comfortable with and the personalities you weren't particularly fond of. Equally, you will have inherited opinions on others based on the thoughts of the people you most respected and trusted. You would have heard statements like "He isn't a good person" or "She isn't very nice." This early conditioning is why you made judgments about people very quickly. Unconsciously, you decide what you think about a person prematurely because you jump to making assumptions on what you think you know about someone. You probably haven't realized how much modeling the behavior of the closest people around you growing up has affected how you think and behave around others today.

Another critical part of your early development was your communication with others through your spoken language. These habitual words are essential when we want to share information with others, but words can also cause plenty of confusion between people because of our interpretation of the meaning we give to them. Most of the words you learnt are by listening to others, whether that's through the education you received or through your upbringing. You would have started to choose words to describe how you felt, what you saw, how you understood a situation, and what you were thinking. Over time, these words influenced and hypnotized you through the meaning you gave them. For instance, you gave everything a name and a label, and with it sometimes a mental image of how you saw it. This habitual nature of labeling comes from your conditioning that everything needs a name and a description for you to understand it better and fully appreciate it. This is how the mind combined your language and thoughts to help you to understand any experience you were going through. Very quickly, you formed an attachment to the need to use these words to make your opinion known and for the validity in what you thought you knew about something. It is because of these early habits of labeling that humans find it so hard to experience anything properly. We love to judge, name, and define everything by using our habitual language to describe what something means to us, rather than being more open-minded.

Another form of your early development was the internal communication with yourself; your constant inner chatter, the part of you that never sleeps, this uninterrupted noise coming from your mind. The inner chatter gets to work very early in your life on creating ideas and beliefs. It is always looking for conflict from what is happening around you, describing your emotions, telling you what you should be doing, and making internal announcements to you when you weren't getting what you wanted. The forever friend working on your behalf to ensure nothing is missed or forgotten by your mind. Imagine how annoying this would be if everyone could hear this inner self-talk, not to mention embarrassing? We aren't conscious of this when we are young, and some humans unfortunately never become conscious of it and go through their lives totally controlled by this voice.

When you were a child, you had this incessant need to ask questions, a kind of curiosity that needs a lot of energy. Children are known to ask all sorts of questions, starting with the famous "Who?", "What?", "When?", and "Why?" You have to admire their persistence at times. They don't like to be ignored and very rarely accept one-word explanations. It is because they are in the habit of learning and this is driven by asking questions. Likewise, questions are an integral part of everyone's lives. Adults are no different to children as to the amount of questions they ask; the only difference is most of the questions an adult asks are internal and designed to sabotage themselves. The mind is always rating everything and looking for reasons why something isn't the way it should be. Every thought, in essence, could be described as a question. Think about this for a moment: every time you have a thought about something, inside that thought is a hidden question that requires an answer and this answer determines how you feel. The type of questions you ask is a reflection of what you experience and these experiences make up your reality.

This continued early development of a human's experience is extremely significant in how they approach life as they got older. For example, if your family struggled with money and this caused unrest and conflict at home, subsequently this would inject a desire and need to have more money in your own life when you are older. Another example is of a child who feels unloved and lonely. They make an internal promise that when they have children of their own, they will treat them with the love and attention they missed out on. Conversely, a child that was loved and treated well would have a positive impact growing up about family life. There are also the examples of parents who are continually arguing and getting upset with one another; as a consequence, this causes the child to feel unsettled, scared, and insecure, making them believe unconsciously that even the people closest to them can't be trusted. In essence, what I'm referring to is that every experience you had as a child growing up has affected, influenced, and created who you are today. During this early period, you went through so many good and bad experiences, which are all influencing how you make decisions and choices today. Even the thoughts and emotions you experienced more often are all a direct result of the drama during your upbringing.

School and your education played a huge part in what you've learned to do. So much of your conditioning comes from your school years. Throughout your time in education you learned and understood more about yourself. Your communication skills grew, and you learnt to interact with other children and became more receptive to playing games and learning new activities. You discovered how to express something you were thinking and feeling in more detail. Your confidence levels grew outside of your typical environment by learning how to adapt to new surroundings. Your early education was essential. However, it wasn't long before you were being judged and categorized based on your perceived intelligence, aptitude, and attitude. I remember several pupils who were very bright but believed otherwise because of what they were told. Therefore, what they believed about themselves was consistent with what the teachers and other pupils believed, and this belief inevitably held them back. I'm sure even today you may have experienced moments when you've been pigeon-holed because of how someone else has judged you. This could be by your parents, partner, boss, work colleagues, and even your friends.

During your school days, you discovered what is required to make friends, what it felt like to be accepted, and how it felt when you were rejected. You also learned about a different type of emotional pain. Children can be cruel unintentionally. Most of the time it is the unconscious behavior for attention, and this can bring out the worst in them. Children that pick on someone else don't always realize the long-term impact this could have on the other child, particularly if this is not the first time; there may have been similar messages received more subtly from others too. Because of my glimpses of witnessing my thoughts very early in my life, I had some empathy for the bully. I saw the vulnerability in the role that was being played out and the need that was being met as a result of what may have happened in their life either in the past or present. Research shows that most bullies have either had a direct experience of being bullied themselves or seen someone close to them being bullied. During your classroom years, you learned about many different personalities. There was the more outspoken and confident child who is usually the one who has more impact on others; however, in a typical classroom, the group is collectively conditioning each other through the time they spend together. Have you heard the saying "birds of a feather flock together"? I don't believe this to be true. It implies that we automatically make an unconscious choice to make friends that are similar to us, but in fact, what we do is build the same beliefs and values over time with them and then confirm we have something in common. Think about some of the habits and behaviors you had as a child, and you will notice many of your closest friends and colleagues also had the same.

As part of your early development, there was the beginning of your habitual nature, the thought patterns you used regularly, your behavioral patterns in specific environments, and your reactions to certain situations. These automatic reactions became part of your identity. You may be known by others as being predictable in certain environments; it's almost like they know how you will behave well in advance. For example, when someone said or did something to you that you didn't approve of, crying and getting upset may have been your emotional response, and this would present itself consistently. You would also have developed some understanding of the habitual nature in others. There would be predictable and habitual responses from your parents and guardians to something you did, good or bad. This could be a kind of punishment you received when you needed to be disciplined or a reward you would receive when you needed to be praised. All habits are part of the same early conditioning which is formed unconsciously and triggered by an emotional response to something from past experience. Humans only become aware of their habitual nature when it starts to get in the way of something they want to do or stop doing. We all recognize people who have bad habits, whether it is with their behavior or thoughts that resulted in them ruining their lives and the lives of the people around them. Everywhere you look, most of the damage in this world is created by people who developed bad habits and didn't know how to break them.

      As you continued with your development, you then started to form a conscious awareness of who you were. You started to identify on a much deeper level what you believed about yourself. You became more opinionated. You thought you had an understanding of what was best for you and as a result were also very conscious of what others thought and believed about you. It is the unhealthy beginning of the personality show. This is when you start to think it is more important what others think of you than your own opinion of yourself. When this becomes natural, you start unconsciously hiding what you don't feel good about and begin feeling the need to lie if necessary. How much of what you believe about yourself or want others to believe about you are lies? How often do you lie on a daily basis, and why? Also, what is your earliest memory of telling a lie? Lies are an interesting part of the make-up of a human being. Humans have learned to lie because they believe it helps them to get what they want and this is something else we learned to do from a very young age. When we were children, we figured lying got us out of doing something we didn't want to do, or out of a sticky situation where we didn't want to get into trouble or suffer the consequences.

Your first real experience of others lying would also have been at school. We all had friends who lied to us just to fit in or impress us, the so-called playground lies. I recall one friend who was a serial liar; we all knew about his life outside of school, but everything that came out of his mouth was either a colossal exaggeration or a blatant lie. This wasn't because he was a bad person, it was because he felt insecure and embarrassed about his own life situation. You too may have been guilty of this. Sadly, it doesn't end in the playground. Humans do this throughout their lives; we have become so insecure that the only way to feel good about ourselves is to have the admiration of other people.

The older we get, the more imaginative we become with our lies. For example, we might be looking for an emotional reaction in someone else in order to get what we want. In a relationship, we might lie about something that didn't happen in our past in order to feel much closer to someone. Humans do this all the time. It's easier to lie than to face up to the truth and risk losing the emotional connection with someone. Lies play a significant role in our lives.

I'm not suggesting we all lie deliberately because we think it's normal and fun to do. Humans lie to protect themselves and genuinely believe it helps them to get what they need, or at least makes it easier for them. Lying is an exercise humans have mastered in order to look good in the eyes of other people. This is how insane the world has become, when we are willing to sacrifice our integrity for the admiration of others. Humans crave attention and will do anything to get it, sometimes even by compromising on their own standards, beliefs, and values—another illustration of how we are caught up in our imagination to create a lasting self-ideal.

Beyond the education you received, you created the obsessive need to learn new things. Humans don't like to miss out on anything, especially anything that is new and may be of value. Humans are always competing at some level for the attention to be recognized for being better than others. This could be for the reward it offers or merely to make sure others know their place against us. Knowledge today is available at your fingertips. We all learn best when we know it is of benefit to us, but most of our learning is "desire motivated" and does not have any lasting value. In fact, too much knowledge is extremely detrimental to what we don't know and believe about ourselves. The roles we create and play throughout our lives require the constant need for learning, which coincides with the unquestionable thirst to reinforce the strength of these roles and our self-image.

We live in a world that believes knowledge is power. Everything is moving so fast in front of us that we are finding it hard to keep up. Technology changes like the seasons; we have to keep updating everything to stay in touch, and we are under constant pressure to learn new things or otherwise we are made to feel we will get left behind. Human beings have a severe amount of learning power and have no limits to what they can do. Unfortunately, most of what you are learning and doing is taking you further away from your true identity. I firmly believe we should learn what is necessary to stay in touch with this ever-changing world, but let's be honest with ourselves and assess how much of what we've learned in the past is benefiting us today. Our minds are filled up with so much unnecessary information which is affecting them. Every day we are being influenced by the media, television, our place of work, friends, and family. Most of it is communicating to our internal voice which has taken control of us. When your focus is on the things that have no real value, what you learn is obstructing your ability to know the truth.

# Remember

You developed an awareness of your environment

---

You began to relate to some emotions, such as fear.

---

You started to develop a habitual language

---

The internal chatter had started

---

The conditioning process was in motion

# Quote

---

"Employ your time in improving yourself by other men's writings, so that you shall gain easily what others have laboured hard for."
**-Socrates-**

---

# Chapter Three:
# Identifying Needs

As your self-perception developed, you began to recognize and identify with your needs and desires. In principle, all your behavior is intrinsically motivated by what you need and desire. The unconscious mind dictates what you need to feel good from your past conditioning. There will always be a belief that you can be better, your circumstances can be better, or the situation isn't good enough. You create what you need and desire based on how you want to feel. This could be about yourself or a situation in your life. Your actions and decisions are all founded on either the need to avoid feeling bad or the need to feel good, and this is governed by how you interpret each experience you go through.

Needs and desires become a constant focus. You have smaller short-term desires which don't require much thinking, and then there are long-term needs that require more meticulous planning. Needs and desires can be defined in many ways. Other than the basic survival needs of food, clothes, and shelter, you have the functional needs for your mental stability and balance. These needs are prioritized based on what you thought was important at any given time for your contentment and peace of mind. There are some which are more integral to creating a mental balance for a human, and without these, we can lose the ability to function correctly. I believe these to be as follows: there is the need to feel safe in the present moment and certain about the future. The question your mind will ask is "How comfortable do I feel in this moment and what will I need in the future to feel secure and certain?" Then there is the need to have a sense of belonging and a need to feel loved. Ultimately, this is the strongest of them all. Accompanying the need for love, humans also have a need to be appreciated and respected. Another need is to feel significant, to have a sense of importance, to be recognized for what they represent and how the world views them.

When you had less dependence on your parents and guardians for your needs, your imagination developed, and you took over the responsibility for what you wanted and needed to feel good about yourself. Initially, most of what you wanted, independent of your home life, was predominantly connected with what took place during your school years, and it is here where most of your needs were met. Mainly, for your mental well-being, there was the need to be accepted by the other pupils. This involved making new friends. You were now at an age where there was enough life experience of people to make an informed judgment of others. You would also have an unconscious understanding that it was necessary to act and behave a certain way to make friends; this was from your first understanding of role playing. You responded instinctively by changing and adapting your behavior around people out of fear of rejection.

The attention seeker was always there; your craving for attention from your parents and family was the beginning, and you did whatever it took to get your fair share. However, the competition of attention got much stronger at school. You may have recognized some traits and skills that set you apart from other pupils, and this then became the primary method you deployed to receive attention.

The student that stood out from others for the capacity to learn often receives the recognition of being smart. The class clown receives attention for being funny and making others laugh. The more athletic student receives attention for being competitive and having a winning mentality. Even the school bullies received their quota of attention from the respect and fear of other pupils. These early experiences of either being accepted or rejected would have a profound bearing on your personality later in life.

During your adolescent years, you started needing the approval of others unconsciously, so you began to become more conscious of the "me". Your priority was to protect the sense of worth you had assembled to date and determine what else was necessary for your future. This was when the personality show took an ugly turn. When you were a child, it was only for your basic needs, but as you got older, it became more interesting; you discovered a desire to be admired and envied. This was the cue for your imagination to get creative and to project a future that would demand admiration from the world, and you started to judge and compare the amount of attention and recognition you were receiving. What others thought and believed about you was beginning to take center stage, and you were willing to compromise your integrity to fulfill the need for recognition.

For recognition, some humans feel the need to lie about their relationships, the amount of money they have, and their achievements, merely to prove their self-worth. As I alluded to in the previous chapter, if the lie was told repeatedly, it is possible for the mind to start believing in its own made-up stories, further confusing it. Let me ask you this: have you ever lied about something because you felt the need at a particular time to feel better about yourself or to get what you want? Everyone lies from time to time. This can be a white lie to protect the feelings of someone or a lie that could have enormous consequences and regrets. We all started the practice of lying during the childhood phase. Children lie to their parents and teachers to avoid being punished for misbehaving or to their friends about anything that makes them look better in their eyes. Humans also make assumptions when in the company of others and decide quickly what they need to lie about to fit in. This stems out of the fear of being rejected and judged. Lying has become part of the human psyche; without lying, humans fear being found out and are afraid of being embarrassed. Humans also lie to get others to do or behave in accordance with what they want. You may also refer to this as being manipulated. Humans have become so afraid of just telling the truth because they are so conscious of what others think that lying has become routine and everyday behavior. The imagination for lying has no limits, and it is the driving force behind the false stories about who they are. To what degree would you lie to get what you want, and how often do you feel the need to?

With age, these needs intensified and became more obsessive; the measures taken by humans can be quite extreme because of the overwhelming need to feel good about themselves and their lives. In principle, all humans' needs are very similar. The only difference between people is how they decide their needs are going to be met. For example, for someone to feel loved, they may simply need to know they have people around them that care. For others, they may need to be told every day that they are special and loved. Similarly, for someone to feel happy, they may need to feel healthy and have their loved ones around them, but for others, they may need a few million in the bank and the recognition that comes with it. There are also the more destructive patterns of behavior where humans act irresponsibly and make bad choices to meet specific needs. On the surface, all they want is for the world to recognize they exist; nobody wants or likes to be ignored. This is the concept of some criminals whose behavior doesn't have any other motive other than the sole purpose of recognition and the need to feel important.

Likewise, all of your relationships are based on needs and what you want from others. Look around and you will see this for yourself; each relationship has its own individual needs, however important it may be to you. If a relationship doesn't meet the needs of someone, it breaks down and loses its value, and conversely, if your needs are being met then the relationship has a strong foundation and every chance of lasting. In fact, the closer you feel to someone, the more needs you have attached to this relationship. One of the closest relationships is that of a parent and a child and is often viewed as unconditional. Yes, there may be a strong bond there, however, both the parent and child do have conditions and rules for the relationship to remain healthy. If either compromises these conditions or breaks the rules, it has been known for parents and children to lose love for each other.

Then we have the relationship with our partner, the person we promise to spend the rest of our lives with, for richer or poorer, in sickness and in health. Consider for a minute the number of rules and conditions set in this relationship. The needs are so demanding that some couples part company just from the pressure of having to meet these needs. At any given opportunity, couples are continually demonstrating and highlighting points of how some of their needs aren't being met. The relationship is full of constant direct and subtle threats. Also, unconsciously, for each relationship you understood the needs of others. Fundamentally, these are specific needs that are your responsibility, and you knew what role was required on your part to fulfill them. Understanding the needs of others rests on how important these other people are in your life and how the relationship would be affected if their demands weren't met. The consequences of not meeting someone else's needs can be stronger than not meeting a similar need of your own. This is because you cannot always influence or change someone else's feelings and thoughts the same way you can with yourself. Humans are terrified of being alone, and for this reason, the needs of the people closest to them may take precedence over their own.

You also have the need to be right. Being wrong is perceived to be negative, and this is another thing which belongs to the family of destructive needs. You are fully aware that the need to be right all the time causes a lot of unrest to your mental state, yet you cannot let go. This is because you think not being right is a sign of weakness, especially if you don't stand up for yourself and back down. There is the belief that you have lost the war of words, and the other person has got the better of you. The unconscious conditioned thought is "They are better than me, and this makes me feel vulnerable." This could possibly mean being belittled, and that you have lost a psychological battle which could lead to negative consequences in the future.

Everywhere we look, people are in conflict with each other for the desire to be right. Understanding one another is the most significant problem humans face today; this is the real epidemic. The conflict and desire to be right is the cause for most of the stress humans suffer. World leaders have been causing conflict between countries because of the need to be right for centuries; millions of people have been killed in the past 100 years with countries going to war for the need to be right. Business people are attacking each other every day through boardrooms to prove who is right, the streets have become unsafe because of the need to be right, and even our own homes are never far away from the next argument over the need to be right. The drama of being right and wrong destroys families, friendships, businesses, and organizations; it divides religions, cultures, and countries, yet it is still so important to us.

Throughout your life, there are also the materialistic needs and desires that make you feel good; all of these objects represent your taste. What you possess and own sends out a message to the world about who you are. Many people like to boast about their possessions to illustrate their status in the world and to demonstrate their personal value, wealth, and success. Everything we decide to purchase may offer its practical purposes, but a vital part of the decision of what we choose is based on the need for the admiration of other people. For example, if you knew in advance of buying something new that nobody else would see it or compliment you for it, the decision of what to buy might be very different. All the best marketing brands and companies are fully aware of this need in humans, the feel-good factor that comes from the recognition and approval of other people.

We may not always be conscious of this, but materialistic needs also become a burden. Something new and expensive needs to be protected. We worry about losing it or it getting damaged. We may even have to get it insured and keep it somewhere safe. Let's be realistic, most of your needs and desires are often short-lived. One day, it is one thing that will make you happy, the next day, it is something else. You keep setting higher targets to make yourself feel good. It is not long before you want a new job, a new partner maybe, new interests, a better house or car, more holidays; it is endless, and all of this is primarily driven from fear and insecurity of what you have created with your mind. Needs and desires always start with the intention of making you feel good, and it isn't long after when they create unnecessary anxiety and stress because of the fear you then have of losing them. The security you are continually chasing, unfortunately, can never be achieved through achievements or the accumulation of possessions. This temporary elation of acquiring and wanting new things is another one of life's traps which you are caught up in, and you cannot escape from this in your present state. The level of consciousness is the problem. You need to rise above it before you can find the key to true happiness.

But which part of you craves these need and desires? Why and what decides this constant unerring pressure behind your needs? And why can't you ever put this flame out? This dominates most of your thoughts; you are either thinking about the next desire or trying to protect what you believe you need to keep hold of. All of this is to satisfy the thirst to feel good about yourself, and this overprotective desire to keep and have what you believe you deserve. The human being can be incredibly selfish and never tires of working and figuring out what it wants to feel good. Deep down, all of us know our needs have consequences, and all the feelings we attach to them subside over time. Once a need loses its value, humans push it away like it was never necessary in the first place. But we still keep creating and striving for more, this continual desire that nothing is ever enough.

Do our needs stem from boredom, the relentless desire to keep doing something out of the fear of missing out, or is it to feel more relevant and better than others? Does the world we live in make these decisions for us? After all, we are continually being influenced by anyone and everything we are exposed to. There are many willing participants in our lives that like to share with us what we need. So are humans a bunch of needs created through our senses and with our minds? Is that what defines us, and is that the reason why we are continually changing as people, because our needs and desires keep changing? I am familiar with some people who believe they are only a means to an end; it's almost like they are always in the process of becoming something more and complete, a product of who they are meant to be, chasing their imagined final outcome. It sounds crazy but many people live this way.

It wasn't until I started experiencing the transient nature behind me that I understood how much impact needs have on how we feel. It is a vicious circle. We thrive on creating new needs. We are gripped by the power our mind has over us and it's a sad reflection of what we humans are doing to ourselves. You have designed something which requires constant feeding to feel good. The tragic part is that you don't even know that your mind is preventing you from true happiness, and this is what keeps you hidden from the truth of who you are.

Needs and desires chain the human to the fear of losing what they have because it affects who they are. The conundrum you face is that you create a need to add to your self-worth, then fear losing the need to protect your self-worth. Wow! How we've been trapped with this battle to fulfill our needs and desires for something we've created with our minds. All of your needs are just assumptions. Your mind confused reality, and it is the mind deceiving nature to keep your focus in the future, making you believe that's where any happiness and peace resides.

# Remember

You started to identify with your needs

---

You developed the need for the approval of others

---

You became more conscious of the "me"

---

You identified how your needs would be met

---

Needs had started to dominate your thoughts

# Quote

---

"What humans want and fear is the same thing, freedom from themselves"
**-Rany Athwall-**

---

## Chapter Four:
## Down Memory Lane

Anything that your mind recorded and remembered when it is called upon, you refer to as a memory. In principle, it is an old thought conditioned by the past. At some point during your childhood, you grasped the concept of time. Realizing this enabled you to calculate and measure your day. Time became your indicator to ensure you were where you should be and to control your daily routine. Time plays a huge role in your life; you've used the clock to function and manage the time you have. As a child, it was your parents, guardians, and schoolteachers who put together your daily and weekly schedule. They decided how your time should be prioritized and determined how much time you had to do something.

Gradually, as you got older, you were given more responsibility over your time. Primarily, time was used on a day-to-day basis, and you had an unconscious understanding and enough life experience of how much of your time was required to complete functional tasks. But with age, time became more psychological; it wasn't purely to use for what you had to do in life, but time was now used to remember what you had experienced in your life. You did this by creating a past and imagination for the future. This is when life gets interesting, and the human mind starts the real work of using time.

Your memory has primarily been a part of your learning experience. Anything you've needed to remember and recall upon is recorded and stored in your memory for future reference. During your life, your memory has helped to keep you safe, away from harm, and it uses your past experiences to prevent you from repeating any mistakes and pains, particularly anything that was associated with physical or mental pain. Equally, it is also there to remind you of anything that was a pleasurable experience so that it can be repeated. Your memory has shaped many of your beliefs, and in the early childhood years, your memory of past experiences played its part in your development. My earliest memories from my childhood are probably from the age of five, albeit vague and limited. I do have some thoughts which have traveled with me throughout my life and, without being specific, influenced what I believe about myself.

You often look into the past for references of what something means and the potential outcome of a considered choice that needed to be made. It is also not uncommon for humans to use references from the past of other people they trust, especially close relationships. You also turn to your past for your self-belief, the place where you keep all of your skills and abilities intact. When in question, you use past examples of how you overcame a particular problem or how you completed a challenge. Your memory also stores any self-doubt you may have; moments when you weren't at your best and when you failed to achieve a particular goal. I'm sure you also have memories you wish you could delete or change, memories of past experiences you aren't particularly fond of and as a consequence may have held you back. This type of memory can have a long-term damaging effect on the mind of a human if they become regular thoughts. Society believes answers to many mental issues and psychological problems can be found by taking a trip down memory lane, searching for hidden clues about how and why something is affecting someone.

However, I don't want to go through the primary purpose and benefits of having a memory. Instead, I'm interested in what you have deliberately retained from your past for who you believe you are and what makes you do this. As you got older, during your adolescent years, you now had a much larger memory bank to reflect on, and your memories became an integral part of your life. You started to make mental notes about your past life story consciously. This is anything and everything you felt was necessary and was to be remembered. Unconsciously, your memory became your trustworthy companion to remind you of who you are, what you have achieved, and what you've learned about yourself, since your story cannot be consistent unless it is remembered.

Similarly, what you chose to remember during your life has had a profound effect on the decisions you made and on your actions. You combined these memories to create a history of your journey, of the ups and downs in your life. As you keep getting older, the more of a past you have to hold on to and work with. Unfortunately, your memories can be very unreliable, especially when it comes to remembering specific details, and is far more fallible then you realize. Information from your past changes when you recall a memory depending on your present state of mind. You also change and adapt your past experiences based on your current needs. Memories are a fundamental part of the mind-self which you have been creating. As alluded to earlier, your memory has its distinct advantages for the experiences in your life and what you learn from them, but it's what you ultimately rely on when you think about who you are and your interpretation of these memories which affects what you believe.

With your past, you use your memory to create a story you want for yourself and something you believe others will be fascinated to hear. Your memory bank is your presentation and the go-to place to impress other people or make them interested in you. Any opportunity to talk about yourself is not to be missed because it makes you feel good about yourself. At times, you may even have glorified and lied about many aspects of your story, especially regarding events that can't be checked or confirmed. A classic example is when humans exaggerate about many of their childhood stories to create a picture that seems better in their mind and the eyes of others. Equally, depending on the conversation, when a person is looking for sympathy, they usually formulate the story to look much worse.

All of these actions are characteristic of how humans use their past to create a more exciting and attractive story today. Nobody wants an uninteresting past and to be considered as boring; it's either fantastic at times or somewhat tragic. Very rarely is it anything in between. This is why humans can be very selective of what they want to remember and describe as their past. Even your inner conversation is influenced by your past. It becomes something of value and needs protecting at any cost. Nobody likes their past to be judged or questioned. As you began developing and recognizing your personal story you relied less on the memories from your past experiences and slightly more on your imagination to create something more stimulating, all very much fabricated and manufactured, with the minimal amount left that is true.

Your relationships are also influenced by your memories of people. Whether it is someone you see every day or only on occasion, each experience with them is a memory, and you choose to keep the memories that you believe to be of most value to you. Through the contact and experience you have with people, you process information about them in your mind and create a personal version for your interest. In fact, you delete what you feel isn't relevant and keep the parts you need to make your judgment of them. Over time, you keep changing and updating what you believe about other people through the experience you have with them, but which version is real, what you think of them or what they think of themselves?

Every role you've ever played and acted out is an accumulation of experiences with memories attached to it. These memories stay with you, but the role acted out continues to change. Your mind then continues to rely on a memory that was connected to a transient role played out at a different time in your life. Let's think about this: a human goes through a number of experiences as a child, and some of these experiences were perceived to be negative and harmful. The role at the time is one of a child, yet the memory still affects the adult many years later, even though the role to now be played out is entirely different. Humans similarly interpret many experiences differently over time because they are connecting several previous experiences and memories to create a present outcome.

As previously mentioned, the mind can deceive you into believing memories that may not be true. Then there is that inner voice of the past script that runs through your mind, interpreting your every action and reaction to someone or an event. This adds to the cocktail of mixed memories and experiences that are defining you throughout your life. What a mess it creates. Is this really who you want to be? A past you vaguely remember, some of it not even true and most of it irrelevant to who you are today, and yet you still have so much faith and pride in your memory about your life. Why do your memories have so much power over you, and why do you trust your memories so much? The obvious answer is that you believe this is who you are, and the only way you can prove you existed through time. It is your personal story and what makes you unique.

# Remember

You grasped the concept of time

---

Memory is primarily part of your learning experience

---

Your memory shaped many of your beliefs

---

With your past, you've used your memory to create a story

---

The mind has deceived you into believing memories that may not be true

# Quote

---

"Everybody is a genius. But if you judge a fish by its ability to climb a tree, it will live its whole life believing that it is stupid."
**-Albert Einstein-**

---

# Chapter Five:
# It's Just a Thought

Throughout your life, you have invested way too much in your internal voice. You are at the mercy of it, and humans are like puppets, acting on its every thought. You have also become susceptible to believing the inner voice is there to help you and therefore believe it is a source of facts and truth. Humans very rarely query its morals and jump quickly to its defense if it is questioned. This inner voice is confrontational and is willing to jeopardize anything good that comes to you by asserting its opinion and deceiving you into believing it has your best interests at heart. You've been using your mind as a computer to rely on the information stored from your personal experiences and memories.

Your mind has become the window of your perception of events. It dictates how you perceive and analyze every scenario and situation, the meaning you give something, and the belief you create from it. Each interpretation has been shaping and creating the world around you from an early age, and unconsciously during your lifetime you have implemented and designed thought patterns and beliefs which have determined how you feel about every outcome in your life. You've created quite a collection of conditioned thought patterns and reactions. You have thought patterns that scare you, that make you feel insecure and uncertain, patterns that get you to feel excited or feel sad. Whatever the thought pattern, it is a part of your mind's past conditioning. From this standpoint, your mind creates random and constant thoughts that run through your head without your permission. Many psychologists state that most humans have on average 70,000+ thoughts a day and nearly 80% are negative. Because of the negative tendencies of the mind, the default setting is to ask negative questions, and in return, your mind comes up with negative answers. Humans have become addicted to negative thinking, and like all addictions, it is a form of self-inflicted suffering. Your mind is continuously rolling out questions and answering them. It loves to create problems and then receive the recognition for solving them. All humans are faced with many difficulties and challenges in their lives.

The concern is that they allow themselves to get carried away by their thoughts. There is nothing unusual about a human reacting badly when things don't go their way, and this is usually followed by making the situation worse because of the bad choices made under this confused state. When our mind is out of control, our thoughts can be dangerous, causing chaos in our lives and playing havoc with our emotions. Inevitably, this brings about more pain and suffering. Sadly, you have become attached to these regular and unpredictable thought patterns that keep churning around in your mind, repeating themselves over and over again without you having any real control to stop them.

You don't have a manual or a book about what each experience should mean. However, every experience you go through leads you to think different thoughts, and the program you are working from in your mind responds differently to every situation depending on how you feel and the environment you are in. This is because you've been adding and interpreting each experience based on the thoughts from previous experiences; this causes a tremendous amount of confusion when trying to understand your reaction to a particular situation. You have allowed your experiences to condition your thinking, and you've come to rely on your mind and thoughts for an explanation for everything you've been through. For the most part, it's been a mixed bag of inconsistent feelings and thoughts. Because of the unpredictable state of your mind, there is no logic applied to your thinking and imagination. Your thoughts about a particular experience change depending on your current state of mind, and you can have the same experience twice and give it a different meaning. Consequently, it doesn't come as any surprise why you've been living with so much confusion about your thoughts and feelings. The constant inner dialogue has made you confused about reality, and your imagination continues to create situations and scenarios of what might happen in the illusion that is your future.

Because of the conditioning of the mind, you also have no control over how your body reacts to these thoughts. When something happens, your body doesn't say, "How should I feel?" or "What thought should I do now?" It is on autopilot and from the mind's past recorded data it chooses a response. Your nervous system is extremely intelligent, but it cannot tell the difference between something you experienced and something that was just a thought. A simple thought without an experience is enough to send a signal that can affect any part of your body: your heart rate, temperature, the ability to control your muscles, even your vision and balance.

I'm sure you've had many experiences of your imagination running wild. You can be anywhere or anything by just having a thought. Look at how quickly you move into the future or the past with a thought. Your thoughts also have the power to make you relive past unpleasant experiences several times over. It's as if once wasn't enough to have a bad experience. Your mind loves to relive past feelings, good or bad. There would also be many occasions in your life when your thoughts made a particular experience feel much worse. This internal dialogue puts the mind in all sorts of states and uncertainty. Over a lifetime, your thoughts are made up of so many fictional and non-fictional stories about you and your life experiences. Most of it is just random bits of edited information from your memory of what you continue to believe about yourself. Your thoughts are very unpredictable and demanding. Remember, every moment in your life is just an experience; it's your thoughts that keep changing, and the meaning you give them. The good news is that you can learn to use thinking constructively. Your mind can be extremely creative and help you to solve any of your life challenges, but many humans don't know how to create a balance between logically thinking. Instead, they allow their thoughts to get in the way and create adverse outcomes in the mind.

Most humans never realize the impact their thoughts are having on their lives. We are in the 21$^{st}$ century and are inundated with self-help books, courses, and seminars for advice on personal and professional development, mental and physical well-being. You may be a person that, through your efforts, has worked on and taught yourself effective ways to think better, especially during times of struggle and stress. Some of us are lucky enough to have a basic understanding, and having some knowledge that can help to improve any aspect of our life, especially if we are committed.

I am a huge advocate of personal development; however, unfortunately, this is not the answer to total fulfillment because some of the methods unintentionally reinforce the belief that you are your thoughts. Another critical challenge that humans discover when trying to understand thought is that throughout their lives, thought has consistently provided some stability to their behavior, whereas anything else is contradictory because it means their behavior has no meaning. The fact that you are more inclined to listen to what you believe, your behavior and attitude, will be a representation of this. It is the nature of your mind to give expression to your thoughts.

You are indeed the architect of your own life, and understanding this is vital to your well-being. Your thoughts don't hold back, and they cannot be trusted. Thoughts drag you down and make your life miserable. For too long, humans have been led by the tendencies of the mind to focus and believe in their thoughts. Your mind is on autopilot, and you have to start navigating it away from the pain it is causing you. Thoughts don't like to stick to facts. Instead, they have a habit of fearing the worst, which in theory is only an illusion. Whilst you live with the notion that your thoughts are to improve your self-image and for the roles you play out in life, the consequences of your thoughts will always end up with disappointment.

When you start making that conscious choice to be more aware of the compulsive nature of thinking and thoughts, you move another step closer to living a life worth loving. Once you are closer to knowing the truth about yourself, a sense of trust and logic appears that will suppress this voice with awareness, and you will no longer trust it. Instead, you will develop a habit of seeing above its noise and nature, and it will be an inward process and a knowing that will be a liberating experience.

# Remember

You believe the inner voice is a source of facts and truth.

---

Your mind is continuously asking questions
and answering them

---

You've allowed experiences to condition your thinking

---

You have no control over how your body reacts
to these thoughts

---

Thoughts don't like to stick to facts.

# Quote

---

"All that we are is the result of what we have thought."
**-Buddha-**

---

## Chapter Six:

## Emotional Impact

How much do you understand about your emotions and what influence have they had on your life? Your body reacts to your thoughts, and this creates a feeling which is referred to as an emotion. An emotion can be a reaction to an event or situation, for instance, something that may have upset you, scared you, or even for those rare moments when something made you feel good. You started to experience emotions from the moment you were born, but when did you begin to understand the emotions you experience more often? More specifically, how have these emotions played a part in your life, and what impact have they had on what you believe about yourself? Some humans become more aware of their emotions than others and try to make a conscious effort to control them.

However, we all realize over time that this isn't easy to do. Predominately, your experience of using emotions in your life has either been to express how you feel about something to yourself and others or when somebody else is demonstrating their feelings and thoughts to you. During your lifetime, negative emotions have always been more prevalent than positive ones. There is fear, anger, sadness, worry, guilt, and frustration, to name a few. Your understanding of these emotions has developed at different stages in your life. When you were younger, you could feel these emotions but wouldn't have necessarily been conscious of them until you started to experience them on a more regular basis or when they started getting in the way of your happiness and peace of mind.

The notorious few that get in the way of your happiness more often are fear, worry, and sadness. Whenever you have had these feelings, it was your body responding to a thought about a situation which you believed to be threatening or potentially harmful. Like all emotions, it is your conditioned beliefs that make you feel this way. It is the anticipation of an outcome based on your previous life experiences that causes you to experience these emotions. They are all a part of your conditioned thinking patterns that create the feelings and not the situation you are fearing. Every time you feel uncomfortable about something and believe it's out of your control, you find it difficult to cope. This is because the problem always lies within you and how you perceive yourself or a particular situation in your life, but you believe it is your circumstances.

Many humans who suffer from constant fear and anxiety are compulsive negative thinkers who see the worst in every situation. This has become their way of dealing with life and they believe this is who they are. We live in an age of people losing their minds, and of having nervous breakdowns; it seems that everywhere we look humans are living with the constant strain of what will become of them. Unattended negative emotions become habitual in a very short period, and they drain your energy. When you focus on adverse outcomes, your thoughts become clouded, and you can very quickly lose control, resulting in more severe conditions such as depression. The reality is, most of your life you have been driven by fear. Behind everything you have and desire is a hidden fear. Fear is also a conditioned belief or a lack of trust you have in yourself.

You may be surprised and encouraged to learn that whilst the inability to deal with fear may feel like a psychological problem, it isn't. From an early age, most of what you were taught was with the threat of something you feared losing. Hence, you now have a belief that fear can be used to drive you to behave a certain way, to push yourself, to motivate you, and to make your life better, partnered with desire. This is a trap, a powerful trap. Desire combined with fear is a dangerous and a destructive combination; there is only one outcome, a very miserable and lonely life. These are the thoughts and beliefs of your conditioned mind. These clever workings are to keep you hooked by living with fear and uncertainty.

Most of the negative emotions deployed regularly can have considerable consequences in your life. However, I believe the most damaging of the negative emotions is anger. How often do you get angry, and when did you realize you had anger in you? Anger is an emotional state that varies in severity depending on how you feel about something. In the early years, you would have noticed yourself getting upset when you felt aggrieved about something, but not angry.

However, as you got older, you became more conscious of the benefits of getting angry when you realized that merely being upset wasn't enough. This is when anger becomes a consistent emotion as a way of showing and demonstrating your disapproval about a situation, person, or an event, and trying to get your way. If adopted regularly, anger becomes challenging to control, especially when you feel offended, misunderstood, accused, judged, frustrated, and many of the other outward-invoked negative experiences. You may have noticed that losing control of your temper doesn't offer any real benefit; in fact, it may have led to many moments in your life that you now regret. I'm sure there have been times when you have been reminded of these occasions, either by someone else or because of a negative consequence of getting angry. Humans have also been known to use anger to demonstrate a sense of power and strength over others, as a form of protection. Anger has a detrimental effect on your mental well-being; the negative energy it has makes you feel low and can lead to other psychological issues. Anger is also the ancestor of violence. We live in a world that is in constant battle because of anger. It is potentially the most dangerous mental state to be in, and one that can have catastrophic results. Anyone who employs the emotion anger regularly is usually responsible for destroying their own life and the lives of others.

Another compelling emotion that controls your feelings is one of guilt, which is at times a complicated emotion to understand. Most people don't know when they are feeling guilty, because it's a painful emotion to break down and understand the mechanics behind, especially when it is with yourself. You may have broken someone's trust or even your integrity, because of your inability to control yourself or a situation; subsequently, you let yourself and others down. Why do humans find it so hard to keep commitments in life, and why do they make so many in the first place? Humans keep compromising their integrity and letting themselves down, demonstrating they are not dependable and reliable.

There will also have been many times during your life when you felt frustrated. Humans have created a hunger for always needing to be doing something with their time to give it value; in other words, there is a feeling that they are on borrowed time and if they aren't achieving something, time is being wasted. Although on the surface we call it "being frustrated", it is the human mind that can't stand still and accept a situation and experience for what it is. Even when you are asleep you are never really still. Your mind is always active and trying to accomplish something. There is a perpetual nature to be doing something. Humans get bored so quickly and frustrated with anything that gets in the way of how they want to feel.

On the flip side, your positive emotions have been doing the absolute opposite. They have been generating positive energy to your body and mind, thus improving your physical and mental health. I'm confident in predicting that the emotion of being happy has been at the top the list of what you would like to experience more often, but why does being happy become more of a challenge as you keep getting older? As a child, you didn't need much to feel happy. Laughing and enjoying life was a regular daily experience. So what happened to you? Was it your life circumstances that removed the joy of living, or was it someone else's fault? At what point did you decide that being happy should be a luxury and something that isn't possible for you to feel all the time? When did you put into place your conditions and rules to feel happy, and why did you think they were necessary?

This deluded thinking is typical of a human that believes they can only be happy when a particular goal or desire has been achieved. This is another example of the conditioning of the mind that makes you think happiness is something for the future. Humans believe unconsciously that happiness is only of value if it is experienced as a reward for some accomplishment. Unfortunately, because of what you believe about yourself, you have trained the mind that happiness is not a permanent state, and instead, you have to find moments of pleasure whenever you can. As a result of this, you have confused pleasure with happiness. You have replaced being happy with the pleasures that life can offer. Sadly, moments of pleasure are limited to time and repetition, which offers its own unique problems.

Feeling good about anything connected to your self-image will in the future offer a negative twist, where there will be a consequence of disappointment. This is because of the expectations you put on how you need to feel; this type of positivity will always have negative connotations within it. For example, a better job with more money will initially make you feel good, however, sometime in the future, the feeling you once attained of receiving the job will dissipate, leaving you with the fear of losing what you gained. The mind's sole concern is to perceive everything with emotion, positive or negative; this is the only way it can judge everything and everyone that surrounds it. Without emotion, how can it tell the story about who you are?

# Remember

An emotion can be a reaction to an event or situation

---

Negative emotions have been more prevalent than positive ones

---

Most of your life you have been driven by fear

---

You have trained the mind that happiness is not a permanent state

---

Your mind is always active and trying to accomplish something

# Quote

---

"If you judge people, you have no time to love them."
-Mother Teresa-

---

# Chapter Seven:
# What's Your Role?

There are so many roles you have become accustomed to playing in your life, some more significant than others, but all of them have a purpose. Some of these roles feel more genuine and less forced than others, and this is founded on the internal roles you act out with yourself. The external roles are usually based on what you want others to believe about you, and the internal roles are based on what you consistently believe about yourself. There is always a discrepancy between the two and many variations on how you interpret them. For both external and internal roles, humans are known to exaggerate what is true to meet the needs of the role. The only difference is that the internal roles acted out can be manipulated by your thoughts, whereas the interpretation of the external role is also determined by what others think and believe about you.

Let's run through a few of the more important roles you played. Initially, there was the role of the child, acted out for and when you were in the company of your parents. This is one of the first roles you unconsciously created, and a very important one. Your parents were often the people you turned to when you needed something, especially emotional support and comfort. The dependency of this role continues to change with age. Your parents would have shared information with you about the roles you played out as a child, which predisposed your beliefs about what you were like, for instance, what you were comfortable with, how you behaved when you wanted something, the primary emotions you used, and with this knowledge your mind built up this self-image of who you were, both positive and negative. You would also have unconsciously mirrored many of the roles they acted out in the company of other people, the way they behaved, certain gestures they used, body language, mainly when associated with a reaction or an emotion. You will also have picked up on the different tonalities and the type of language they used more predominantly. And by default, their role-playing would have a significant influence later in life on how you acted out specific roles yourself.

Parents also play and act out roles with their children. This is never seen purely as a function but continually as a role created in their minds of what they should be doing to serve the child in their own best interest. This stems from the belief that they know what's best and it is their responsibility to ensure the needs of both the child and parent are being met. Naturally, the parent is there to protect the children from harm and look after them, but it never stops there; they create another sense of self by extending their role as parents, rather than merely a responsibility of care to the children. The parent is known to act out many of their desires and needs through their children. Many influence the children's thoughts and beliefs by playing out specific roles to convince them to behave a certain way. Although the love of a parent is often seen as unconditional, beneath this, there is a motivation that the child must adhere to all of their wishes and not disappoint them. The parent creates another part to their own self-image through their children.

Another familiar role you played out in life is that of a pupil and a friend. You went to school to learn and develop your knowledge across many subjects. It wasn't long before you were being judged, assessed, and compared to other pupils by your teachers. Every day you were being influenced on what you thought about yourself based on the beliefs of others, whether you were seen to be a bright student or someone who struggles; you were labeled, tagged, and given a role to act out consistently. An example of this is the pupil who seems to be quiet and isn't intentionally seeking any attention from others, and this pupil is considered to be shy and often becomes a target to be picked on by the other children because they don't represent a threat. This type of categorization is a prime example of how a young child becomes influenced and falls into a role unconsciously because of what someone else believes about them. Any consistent behavior you received at school, either from other pupils or the teachers, developed a belief about yourself, and you routinely played out the role that the moment required. This is part of your early classroom conditioning based on your personal experiences. We also create roles unconsciously to meet the needs of someone else. A classic example of this is the role of the school bully. This role involves being superior by using threatening behavior and this was a way of making sure everyone knew their roles. The role created consciously by the bully was also unconsciously creating another role for the person being bullied: the role of a victim. It is difficult sometimes to figure out which role was created first.

Growing up, we weren't a wealthy family. My parents had to work very hard to make ends meet, but looking at us from the outside, this wasn't obvious. Not intentionally by me, but my friends and other students thought I came from a wealthy family because of where we lived and how I presented myself. My parents always made sure we had everything we needed and more. Back then, I wasn't going to change anybody's opinion about me because it worked to my benefit. You may also have been through some similar experiences where you either intended or unintentionally created an identity built up from other people's assumptions. This isn't a huge problem at first. The challenge is when you become so accustomed to the role that you now fear losing the status it offers if you were found out. This then becomes an uncomfortable pressure and burden to uphold.

When I was seventeen, something happened that tested my resolve. My father was admitted to the hospital with a serious condition. He passed away within a few weeks of his illness. This had a huge and sudden impact on our lives, and for the first time in my life, I experienced a level of uncertainty. Some of my family members understandably took this very hard. However, I didn't experience many emotions; at the time, everyone thought it must be the shock and that people deal with death differently. But I knew that wasn't the reason why I didn't feel the loss as strongly as everyone else. I had my moments in the following months of expressing the loss internally, but there was something else that took over. My early feelings of duality made me feel as if I had just witnessed this experience, and it wasn't something I personally went through. It felt like I was playing out the role required at the time of a son who lost his father. It did make me feel guilty and made me question my feelings towards my dad, and it wasn't until many years later, after I fully understood the human condition, that the subtle messages I was experiencing during my younger years started to make any sense.

As you moved towards adulthood, there were a number of roles you decided to let go of because they were no longer fulfilling any needs. Conversely, some of them were adapted to hold on to the memory that each role once represented. The roles you now started to create were influenced by what you needed in the future in order for you to achieve what was necessary for your happiness. These roles were designed in your mind and this is where you could see them being played out, like a rehearsal in your head or a vision of your future. It could be the role of parent one day, the desire to have your own family, a husband or wife, someone you could share your life with, a professional role like a doctor, lawyer, or accountant, or maybe to run your own business and be the boss. In essence, what you need or needed in the future to be happy is all based around the role of identity it will give you. Once attained, the goal itself often loses its value, but you now have a role identity to preserve, and this can become stressful. An example of this is when you have a desire to be successful at something and believe this new identity is going to change your life and make you happy. Once you achieve the desired outcome, the novelty of what you gained quickly wears off and now the only thing that remains is the pressure of the role identity that was created, and you're left with the fear of losing the self-worth that made you happy.

You have created so many roles to meet the needs for so many different environments and other people in your life. Some of these may not be significantly different, but they are all nevertheless unique in their own right. Humans have a unique role for their partners, children, siblings, parents, friends, work colleagues, and even the boss. Your role determines how you think, speak, and behave in their company, and in return, they will have their interpretation of the role you are acting out, for every person you know from your past and present sees a different you; they interpret your role through their perceptions and experiences of you. In reality, your understanding of other people isn't just two-way, it is four-way, because you see yourself as one role being played out and you interpret a role being played out by the other person. They, in return, relate to the role they are playing out and interpret another role from their perspective of you. It can make understanding one another very difficult at times.

In each relationship, you have been acting out fictional characters to meet your needs and the needs of the other person. Many of these roles have continued to change throughout your lifetime, and you are always having to design and create new versions depending on the circumstances. There is nothing wrong with playing out the different roles for whatever the situation requires from you because you need to be flexible when interacting with different people. The problem is that when you start to identify yourself with these roles, your already extensively confused mind ventures deeper into the hole you have dug yourself into. You rely on that voice of the role inside your head that tells you how you should act to get what you want. Some of us have a misconception that this voice is helping us to get what we need. Unfortunately, most of the time, it doesn't operate logically because it is only interested in protecting the role.

Ask yourself this question: have you been creating roles consciously, or did you happen to fall into them from your life experiences? Acting out the roles we create has become an essential part of the game of life for humans. We've already discussed some of the earlier roles we play, but as we go through life, we adopt and practice so many. Look around you and you will notice the world is full of people acting out roles, believing this is who they are and what they represent. Humans love the roles they play out because they enjoy the drama life offers. All roles played out by you are motivated by fears, rewards, pleasure, and the need to avoid pain. Every role has its equal importance until the role becomes vulnerable or loses its value to you. Then the role becomes a burden, and you try to lose it. In the earlier chapter, we spoke about the needs of a human and how a person is prepared to do whatever it takes to receive attention and recognition. It's fair to say people are willing to settle and play out whatever role is required for admiration, even if it is negative. The world is full of stories, past and present, about people who are acting out evil roles in return for attention and to feel significant. How many millions of lives have been lost throughout the history of humanity where people have succumbed to the desire for recognition of the role they wanted to create?

So why do we create so many roles that we want to portray? The answer is simple. We believe these roles help us to get what we want to make us feel good about ourselves. Do we believe they help to protect the image we've created in our minds? Remember, all of the roles you play out are temporary, and only last as long as they are needed for you to feel good about yourself and your life. We have to control this endless cycle of creating new roles for ourselves before we lose ourselves in them so much that we can't see or believe anything else. The continued existence of these roles relies upon what you feel you need now and what you will need in the future. Unless this changes in you, you can never release yourself from the attachment and weight of the roles you've created in your mind. It is this compulsive thinking that works with your imagination to create roles, and this is the cause of your problems. They are never the solution. You have the ability to do whatever the moment requires without the constant need to create new roles.

# Remember

There are many roles you act out

---

Initially, there was the role of the child

---

You have been influenced on what you thought about yourself based on the beliefs of others

---

You also create roles unconsciously to meet the needs of someone else

---

We believe roles help us to get what we want and make us feel good about ourselves

# Quote

---

"We do not describe the world we see.
We see the world we can describe."
**-Rene Descartes-**

---

# Chapter Eight:
# The Complete Project

There is a time in your life when you have a vague understanding of what is needed to feel complete. It involves looking into the future and deciding what it would look like and how this would make you feel. The questioning self perceives itself in time and therefore looks for the future to feel complete, believing this is what the future is for. It is usually an attempt to cover up an underlying fear that the future might be worse than the present or the present isn't good enough. Humans are always looking to find themselves, searching for ways to feel more complete about themselves and their lives, suggesting it's something they need to keep doing or that something needs to happen for them, whether this is through more personal achievements, more possessions, or just more future. So much combined hope and desire is required on your part to make the finished article.

You want to be respected, loved, admired, appreciated, needed, and you want to have total control of the events and circumstances in your life. In order for this to happen, you have identified some missing pieces of the jigsaw. In your early adult years, you started to define and shape what was needed for you to feel complete by being more specific. The picture in your mind became much clearer based on the potential of what you were capable of achieving, thus making the vision of the future you wanted more probable. The world also presented its opinion about you many times for you to base your expectations on. Likewise, you had a good understanding of your own beliefs and values of what you wanted to avoid in your life and what you believed would make you happier. Your idea of what is possible for you may also have been formed based on how you perceived the experiences and personal achievements of the people closest to you; if it was possible for them, then it was possible for you too. Moving on, you mentally boxed off what was more relevant to you and what required more of your attention. Humans do this throughout their lives by judging various aspects and focusing more on what's missing in the lives, instead of what they have.

There are a few examples of the stages of where a human might be in the spectrum of feeling complete. Some people are only one step away from feeling complete; for example, the missing part may be the perfect life partner, a soulmate they can love. A family of their own, or maybe a more fulfilling job and career that they are handsomely rewarded for. It may even be the new home they've always dreamt of, or maybe it's to lose weight and feel healthier, or even free time to do the things they enjoy. The list goes on and on. Others may still feel a million miles away from being complete, and they have also given up. The reality has set in and they have consciously decided to move the goalposts because they have doubts about their original plan. Look around you and you will notice people who have managed to feel closer to having everything they want, and usually begin to spend more time on what is missing from their lives.

A classic example is that when someone achieves a level of success in one area, they begin to take more pride in other areas, whereas others who don't feel good about many things lose focus even on the things that once represented something of value in their lives. There are also some humans who discover how fragile life can be and feel they can't be bothered anymore because they've come to the realization that even by them achieving everything they set out to do, it wouldn't take much for it all to collapse.

Conversely, it doesn't take much for the cracks to appear in the mental picture of being complete and they lose all hope of ever getting it right. When this happens, humans end up hedging their bets and playing the game of risk versus reward since they don't want to waste any more time on something they don't have much confidence in lasting for very long. They now become more selective and begin to search for a primary purpose to remove any pressure they were under in the past to make life perfect. Some enter the search for religious concepts, and others try to find something that may give their lives more meaning. There are the few that convince themselves it is someone's else's duty to finish off what they started. Unfortunately, these people never applied themselves fully because they were of the belief that it wasn't ever down to them.

Some humans also stop altogether as they are frightened of looking into the future because of past disappointments, and they don't like what the mind has to offer. Equally, to feel better about themselves, there is always the option to shift their focus onto other people's shortcomings to feel more complete by making them less complete. It's still a more comfortable option to judge other people's lives, but humans don't realize when they do this to others they are more likely to judge themselves and the choice to do this ultimately moves them further away from ever feeling good.

But why does it end up like this for so many? Why do you see most people in the world just end up living abject lives, always expecting and planning for the worst and managing their expectations to avoid disappointment, giving up on being happy and seeing the worst in every situation? It should be clear by now that what you need to feel complete is only a part of your imagination and your mind's way of keeping you entrenched in the belief that the present isn't ever good enough and to keep you in the future. This communication is based on its need to protect your future existence and it will discard any threat from you to ignore its needs.

The inherent behavior of someone looking into the future to be complete is to ensure there is some time left in their lives. It's almost like they have added to this need by making time their friend. You cannot ever be complete. Anything and everything you have in your life that makes you feel good about yourself will eventually end. It is all temporary, and therefore everything we chase has a shelf life and will ultimately dissolve. You are continually juggling way too much at any given time, and the more you desire or add to the overall picture of completeness, the less chance you have of ever feeling complete, even if it's only for a short time. If you continue living and thinking this way, you can never be free from the constant striving and searching for those final pieces to complete the picture. It is the design and workings of the mind. You have already spent too much time in your life shifting your focus to what is missing, searching for those final pieces that keep eluding you. Occasionally you think you are getting close, or you may even feel complete for a short time, and then something else goes wrong. It is and always will be a bottomless pit in the search for your completeness. If you fail to see this, you will never be fully content. Instead, you will remain miserable and disappointed.

# Remember

The self perceives itself in time and therefore looks for the future to feel complete

---

It doesn't take much for the cracks to appear in the mental picture

---

There is the belief that the present isn't ever good enough

---

Looking into the future to be complete is to ensure there is some time left in your life

---

You keep searching for those final pieces that keep eluding you

# Quote

_____

"A great man is always willing to be little."
-Ralph Waldo Emerson-

_____

# Chapter Nine:
# Life's Big Questions

You've been asking questions throughout your life. Your mind has been doing this from the moment you learned to speak, and the proverbial inner chatter started. Questions are a vital part of our communication and growth as human beings. Without the ability to ask questions, how would your mind and brain give you the answers to function properly? As a child, it was your inquisitive nature, the need to learn, and you never held back on anything you wanted to know. As you got older the need continued; however, it was now the need for more knowledge instead of the need to learn. Both are of course the same, but knowledge sounds more valuable. There is an unremitting need for knowledge that humans are addicted to. I believe it comes from the fear of making wrong decisions, from the fear of being left behind in this ever-changing world, and the desire to remain one step ahead of the competition. In essence, all of your thinking is based around questions. When you have thought, there is always a question that lies somewhere in the background.

But when did you start asking those uncomfortable questions about life and what purpose do these questions have? I believe it's when most humans are approaching middle age. This could be much earlier for some; nevertheless, it's usually after they have experienced most of what life can offer. They've been through the education process, many of the friendship cycles, experienced the more intimate relationships, acquired the work/career experience, possibly started a family, seen some of the world, achieved a handful of those goals and desires set out earlier in life, and even managed to squeeze in a few hobbies and interests. Emotionally, they've done some learning too, created a history and a past with some good and bad memories. Furthermore, they have created a strong self-image from their beliefs and values, and developed an understanding of what they believe others think and feel towards them. The personality is fixed in place, and they need a few final pieces of the jigsaw to feel complete. Almost there! But then they are hit with some of life's "big questions". People who go through this period of asking more profound questions and in search of answers about their lives, in general, are often described as going through a "mid-life crisis". It's a little unfair to call it a crisis; I'm sure we all have times when we are unsure about who we are and the purpose of our lives. What are these questions? I've gone through a few I believe to be more common later in life.

Let's observe these questions in more detail. One of life's big questions is "Have I managed my time well, and how much time do I have left?" This question involves thinking about the choices and decisions you made throughout your life and, depending on how much time you have left, considering whether there is anything that needs changing. For instance, should you start to look at how you prioritize what you are doing with your time? Maybe you feel the need to be more selfish, and any future decisions should be more in line with what is more important to you. There are phases in everyone's life when their responsibilities require more of them, and when they have to place other people and situations in their lives first. But with time being at a premium, you now may be thinking more about looking after and prioritizing your own needs with the time you have left.

Another group of questions are "Have I achieved everything I set out to do?" or "What have I achieved that is meaningful?" What are my successes and failures? How can this be defined? You may already have some idea and direction of your life's purpose, but you are questioning some of your choices, or maybe you are still in the unknown and searching for something new. You may perhaps reflect on some of those career or business decisions, for instance, did you take enough risks, and is there anything you could have done differently at the time in question? Equally, you might even question whether the failures were significant and whether it was those moments in your life which held you back from being more successful and fulfilled. There may well be many other decisions that indicate you haven't achieved everything you wanted from your life, like the need to contribute more to the broader world by helping people who are less fortunate than you.

"What are my regrets in life?" is another question that often pops up in later years. Regrets can vary from anything you haven't done and wish you had, to something you did do and wish you hadn't. It might be a moment of madness when emotion took over, or just being in the wrong place at the wrong time. Maybe there was someone you cared about and loved that is no longer in your life, and you wished you had shared and expressed your feelings to them more often. Maybe you've spent too much time working, the long hours and days, and there was too much focus on your business or career, chasing the dream at the expense of spending more time with your family and loved ones. Perhaps you have regrets about a dream you had when you were younger and the fear of failure stopped you from taking action and fulfilling this desire. You may regret not taking more care of your health by falling to the temptations of overeating, drinking, and not exercising enough. Or were there other habits you formed that harmed your life and those closest to you? Perhaps there was a decision that carries the burden of guilt that you've struggled to live with or even a person you invited into your life that you now regret.

Another common question is "How will I be remembered?" Humans discover so many ideas and ways to ensure they can still exist in the minds of other people after they are no longer here. It all comes from the fear that this life is all they may have. After all, humans themselves cannot guarantee their existence after death, so they look for ways that they can live on through other people. For some, it might be through the work they've done, how they left their mark on an industry, or through their profession. For others, it's with their possessions and the assets they will be leaving behind for their families. Many even hold on to their beliefs and values, believing this can be expressed for many years after through the people they have influenced. It all stems from the desire and need to leave a legacy of some kind so they will never be forgotten.

The question "Why does it feel like something is still missing?" is an interesting one. You've followed what you felt you needed in your life to be happy, committed yourself to everything that was required of you, ticked most of the boxes, but you still aren't feeling content, and your mind asks, "Is this all there is?" It is typically when a person starts searching for more about who they are, and this can lead them towards the search for something they can believe is bigger and better than themselves to give their life more meaning. It could be either from their religious beliefs or from another believable concept. It's that quest for something more permanent and not something short-lived, as everything else has been in life.

Another big question is "What is the meaning of life?" There is so much that one person goes through in life, but what is it all about? Have we been sent down to earth for a test? Is it a punishment or reward of some kind? Are we born to have an experience of life and then we die, forgotten about over time as if we didn't even exist? Does it mean we were sent here to be judged and selected for what lies ahead after we die? Could our religious beliefs provide us with a satisfactory answer, or older generations, who have stronger, more grounded beliefs? You might be someone who would prefer to ignore this question because there is too much uncertainty and fear that surrounds it.

Whatever answers your mind gives you at the time of asking, they don't always sound convincing, and the questions never go away. We may even turn to our family and friends to provide us with some answers and accept anything that seems more believable and genuine to us. Nevertheless, it can make us feel uncertain about our beliefs on life. These questions can be impossible to answer for most, and they often get ignored or brushed under the carpet because we don't have and can't find any suitable answers. It is difficult to avoid asking these questions because it makes humans feel like life was a complete waste of time and effort because it was never quite enough, and why even bother with this temporary arrangement? A final question, and one I believe is probably the most common that humans ask towards the end of their lives: "If I had the chance to live my life again, what would I have done differently?" I'm confident that most humans have something they would like to change or wish they would have done differently, but whatever questions the end brings to your attention, unfortunately, life itself as you know it can never be enough or perfect.

# Remember

Questions are a vital part of our communication and growth as human beings

---

There is an unremitting need for knowledge that humans are addicted to

---

The uncomfortable questions that need answering keep emerging

---

Whatever answers your mind gives you at the time of asking, they don't always sound convincing

---

Unfortunately, life itself as you know it can never be enough or perfect

# Quote

---

"You have the power over your mind - not outside events.
Realize this, and you will find strength."
**-Marcus Aurelius-**

---

# Chapter Ten:

# Is This the End?

Death is one of the few guarantees you have in life. During your life, there are many moments when you are reminded of death. It could be because someone you know has died or you've heard about the death of someone else. You have had various thoughts regarding death throughout your life. I could argue that everything you do, think about, and experience is in some way connected to death or the fear of it. Think about this: your number one purpose and priority is to protect yourself and the need to survive. Underneath most of what you fear is the inevitable outcome that one day your life will end and the self you invested in will be defeated; the end of life as you know it. So how can you truly ever ignore the question of death? It's impossible.

During your younger years, perhaps you were kept away and protected from having thoughts about death, but as you get older, it becomes more and more difficult to shield yourself from death, especially as you witness so many more deaths that may affect you directly. My first glimpse and understanding of the human condition came from the fear that one day, I would die and no longer exist; this fear consumed me for many years. Many people don't enjoy discussing the subject and details that surround death. It is regarded as a sad and morbid subject, best left alone. In fact, most humans, during the best years of their lives, are only interested in what happens whilst they are alive. The question of death doesn't arise until they are much older. However, there comes a time for us all when the thought and questions surrounding death become more relevant, and there is the need for an appropriate elucidation.

What do you fear about death? Humans have many disparate fears that surround death, but there is always one which you can describe as the primary fear. For instance, some humans' primary fear of death is what will happen next. The uncertainty of not knowing is stressful for humans to live with.

Another primary fear is having to leave so much behind; the people in their lives, their possessions, wealth, and their life story. Equally, there is the fear of death that comes from losing loved ones, should they die first. Or the fear of how death may be presented to them. Will it be an accident, an illness, old age, or something much more tragic? How does death affect your thoughts, emotions, and behavior while you are alive? It is, of course, based on your beliefs about death. The closer you feel to the expectation of the death, the more prominent the influence it can have on your choices and decisions. Ask yourself the question, "How does death affect me, and how many decisions have I made during my life based on my beliefs about death?" You may have decided to look towards your religion or faith for an answer, which could necessitate adopting and following a set of rules dictated by these beliefs. Equally, your moral compass may be questioned when you have thoughts about death, the good and bad you believe about yourself. Death may also bring you a sense of relief, knowing life isn't forever, and maybe there is something better to look forward to.

Perhaps death is a concept to keep you focused in life, knowing you only have so much time to live and you shouldn't waste it. Or is it designed to keep you in line, so there is something to fear, the consequences for the life you've lived? One thing is for sure: the question remains, and everyone needs to select an option or a belief at some point to feel comfortable and content with the inevitable. What are the choices when it comes to dealing with this unknown? It is a question you have decided to avoid and ignore because it is too uncomfortable to answer, or have you chosen to face up to the reality of death and found a suitable solution that you are comfortable with? Everyone has their own beliefs surrounding what happens at the time of death, but there are a few standard views, albeit several variations with all. I believe these to be as follows. The first is that death is the end. When we die, we die; there is no more of the person and no further existence in any other form either. You could call the people who believe this atheists as they also don't believe in a god or anything else after death. For these people it is much easier to believe they are a self which is created through their life experiences and this originated from birth and will cease to exist after death.

Another belief is the heaven and hell concept. This is where God judges humans following their death, and it is then decided where they go. If they have lived a relatively honest and decent life, the gates of heaven will open for them to rest, or if they have committed evil deeds then the fires of hell await. Another common belief is that a human takes on another form when they die and continues this journey, and some believe this is where humans are reunited with loved ones that were lost during their lifetime. All of the aforementioned options are equally believable, as there isn't any real proof presented to anyone to suggest any different and we certainly don't know of anyone that has been through the process of death and returned to tell the story.

Humans define themselves through what they have achieved and experienced throughout their lives and by their beliefs and values, but whatever we do or achieve, somewhere underneath the layers of thought, the question always lingers, who are we and why are we here? So what is it all about? Is this human existence some freak creation that doesn't have a meaning? We are just born to have life experience, and then we die? The mystery behind life and death is probably the most intriguing of questions, and the most avoided. The uncertainty and fear cause humans to behave in peculiar ways. This question can consume your attention at any time. It may be after you've suffered an ordeal or tragedy in your life or when life doesn't make any sense and you have realized how fragile it can be.

Whatever your thoughts on life and death and however you find some peace and relief from the suffering surrounding this fear, the respite is usually only for a short time, and unfortunately, you never get close to understanding or believing anything for very long. You are soon back in your day-to-day story, until the next time an external trigger raises the question again about life and death. Ask yourself this question: "How can I understand life and death when I don't fully understand who I am?" Once you discover the truth for yourself, death becomes irrelevant. You will no longer be searching for answers. Instead, death becomes just another experience for you to go through, and one without any fear.

# Remember

Death is one of the few guarantees you have in life

---

Underneath most of what you fear is the inevitable outcome that one day your life will end

---

There is always one primary fear that surrounds death

---

Somewhere underneath the layers of thought, the question always lingers, who are we and why are we here?

---

Most people unfortunately, never get close to understanding or believing anything about death for very long

# Quote

---

"Yesterday I was clever, so I wanted to change the world.
Today I am wise, so I am changing myself."
**-Rumi-**

---

# Part 2

# Chapter Eleven:

# Let's Reflect

Now that you've read Part One of the book, let us reflect on what has been happening and about what you believe. You started in life by fulfilling a desire and need for someone else, your parents. For identification, you were born with a physical appearance that was unique to you, which continued to develop and change throughout your life but remains unique to you—followed by the understanding that you belonged to a group of people, your family. Soon after, you figured out that there were some other components to what you possessed; collectively, that is. A home, a specific environment, and various material items you could call "mine". Recognizing this was your first step into creating an identity for yourself. It was the foundation of creating a self through a connection with people and objects. Furthermore, as a child you adopted most of the values and beliefs from your parents. This includes their interpretation of the experiences you went through. You developed into a product based on what your parents or guardians taught you and their version of who you should be. It signifies that you weren't born with anything other than your physical body, appearance, and a survival instinct. Remember, no thought came with you into this life, and you were without any mental perception of a self.

    The next part of your life was the learning and mirroring phase. Naturally, you are learning all the time, but the childhood phase of learning is key to how you would interpret your experiences later in life. These were your best years for education since you were using the innocent, clear mind that had only retained a limited version of what you believed about yourself. Instead, when you're older, you are learning conclusively through the self your mind has already created. No longer was it just the mind that was doing the learning, but the identity it had created.

Mostly, what you learn in life is unconscious, and the sole purpose of knowledge is so you can competently function in this world, nothing more. However, as your mind continued to record your experiences, the self you were creating with your mind became attached to what had been learned, adding to its individuality. It is what your mind was already conditioned to do; instead of something being an experience, the mind was interpreting each experience and creating an identity for you. During this stage, who was doing the learning? Was it the empty, clear, and pure mind you were born with, or what the mind had already started to create? Were you now becoming a spin-off from the younger version your parents and guardians created? With some years of recorded data from life experience and the environment you were in, your mind started to unconsciously create an identity for you based on how you interpreted, reacted, and sensed anything you experienced. This was the first real phase of your conditioning.

In the following years, you defined to some extent how the world perceived you, and this became very important, as you needed to know how you were portrayed and what needed protecting. The primary focus now was to preserve what the mind had created and to guard against any outside attack. The self you were creating also had to decide what was needed in the future for its survival. You used examples and references from other people's lives and the level of recognition they received to figure out what was possible for you. It became a staged show, demonstrating and advertising what you stood for. It was important that the outside world knew that you existed and what was unique about you. This mind-created self also discovered specific needs. Rules and conditions were put in place to establish what was needed to be happy, what was needed to feel loved, how to overcome uncertainty, how to have a sense of belonging, and how to be sure about the future. Once your mind defined what was needed, you then mapped out how you were going to fulfill these needs and the type of roles you would need to play for them to materialize. All of this is added without confirmation, a new potential mind self version of what was possible and how you would see yourself in the future. Now added to what the mind had already created were personal needs, more substance on top of substance to create a more specific ideal, all thought created and manufactured by the mind for you to believe in. It is not who you are. It is just an extended version with more life experience and something that now has needs for the mental picture to survive in the future.

Then there is the emotional part. You had a basic understanding of some emotions. Naming the frequent few, you knew what it was like to feel scared, worried, sad, angry, embarrassed, nervous, frustrated, guilty, happy, and excited. You attached yourself to these emotions and began to distinguish yourself through them. You developed an understanding of what made you feel good and what caused you to feel bad. Again, each emotion was interpreted based on how you needed to feel. It was the continuation of the conditioning process and how you used these emotions for identification. Instead of accepting emotions as a reaction of the body, you made them into another part of this so-called "I am". Emotions and thoughts are all conditioned responses from your life experiences. They aren't something that can be controlled by what your mind has created. Attempts were made to manage them, but something that isn't real cannot control them. Thoughts appear randomly from your mind's recorded data. Thoughts run through your mind without your consent. They have nothing to do with who you are; they are just thoughts that appear on an ad hoc basis triggered by past experiences or an imagined future. They aren't who you are.

Moving on, you now had a bundle of memories you could rely on to prove your existence. Memories play a huge part of what you use the mind for. Memory is made up of thoughts carried through time. The older you get, the more memories you have and the more you hold on to deliberately. Some of the memories can be helpful, but there is the part of the memory which your mind-created self cannot afford to let go of. These are the memories you rely on to remind yourself of who you are. Memories are vital for the story to continue; without them, there is the risk that what your mind created would dissolve. Humans love to talk about their past, the stories of when they did this or that, what life was like back then, the challenges, the good times, the achievements and the failures, what they had to go through to get where they are today, and how the past has created the self that is today. It is typical behavior to ensure your survival. Without memories, how can you ever exist in your mind? You must have a past or how can the story remain? Now let's add memories to the self your mind created, some vivid, some vague, some forgotten, some interpreted differently, some even made up, but all in the past, and they only survive because of the mind. It's not who you are. They are only past experiences which you remember, nothing more.

As you moved into adulthood, you deliberately inherited more responsibilities, and the roles you acted out daily had become an essential part of the game of life for you. The roles are made up from life experiences and for the opinions of others. So many roles have been created for so many different environments, and each role determines how you think, speak, and behave in the company of other people. In return, they have their interpretation of the role you are acting out. Every relationship is a role you act out daily, with family, friends, work colleagues, bosses, and neighbors. Many of the roles have continued to change throughout your lifetime, and you are always having to design and create new versions, depending on your needs and the needs of others.

All of the roles you play out are temporary, and only last as long as they are needed to enhance and glorify yourself and your life story. The roles' continued existence relies upon what you think you need now and what you will need in the future. Unless this changes, you can never release yourself from the attachment of the roles you've created in your mind. The roles you have identified with unconsciously through the mind are made-up versions of the self and they are ever-changing based on the environment and circumstances. All roles are made-up fabrications by the mind to support what you believe you need. None of them are real.

With age, you started to rely more on what the future would bring and what was missing from life. You never felt complete because the mind created something that is not real; it's all just a fictional story. This self the mind created cannot live forever when it isn't real. It is created through life experience only. The story is not who you are. You must stop relying on the story to make yourself feel real and complete. The created self is just an experience interpreted with the mind, using thought to give it meaning and life. When you try to explain who you are, you are describing life experiences, interpreted with thoughts and emotions.

Moving on out of fear from total extinction, you started asking the big questions about your life, after going through so much and enduring all the uncertainty life offers. You still feel lost and empty. What you need is some answers. From the time remaining you began to fear the potential outcome and wanted to ensure you had done enough to justify your existence and to ensure you would be remembered. Throughout life, you have never felt content long enough to remain happy, and out of frustration, you start searching for an adequate explanation. It is the insanity of what the mind has created and its need to keep what it took so long to create.

This mind version of you has absolutely nothing to do with who you are. It is all thought created from your life conditioning and from the illusion of time. Finally, as your life reaches the final chapter, the story is nearly coming to an end, and you start contemplating death. The concept of death is met with whatever you feel comfortable with. The self your mind created wants to live on and goes in search of what it can offer after the inevitable since this could mean the end. It lives in the hope that it may be remembered for its achievements, successes, the good it did, or the mark it left on the world. Out of confusion, you need to know there was a purpose to your life. However, it was perceived; in the end, this mind-made version of you is only interested in preventing its permanent annihilation.

To clarify, you were born with a mind totally free of any content. It came with no instructions or manual on how to operate it.

Without your knowing, it went to work unconsciously, developing and creating you and your life. However old you are today, you have been operating through this amazing tool with very little input. Everything you've learnt, experienced, and had a thought about is interpreted through your mind. You weren't born with a self-concept or any perception of who you are; you allowed your mind to get to work from day one in its relentless pursuit to create an identity for you. It did this by using what you experienced in your life and how you were influenced by your environment and people around you.

During your lifetime, the mind has continued to combine your experiences, thoughts, and emotions to design what you believe about yourself. Your very own software program, which you refer to as "ME". Ask yourself this question: "How can I be just an experience?" It is ludicrous to believe you are a bundle of experiences, thoughts, and emotions that your mind holds onto. You have identified with the world of substance. Your mind has connected you to your experiences and come up with a limited version. Is this who you want to be, a mind that has derived an identity from a past you vaguely remember, thoughts that are mixed up at the best of times and aimlessly run through your mind without any consent, experiences that have many different interpretations depending on your state and environment?

It is total lunacy to believe this is who you are, a self created by your mind. You are not your name, title, status, profession, skills, abilities, behaviors, habits, reputation, wealth, health, likes, dislikes, strengths, weaknesses, insecurities, beliefs, values, culture, or religion. This is all made up from past life experience and interpreted through thought. Understanding this dimension of your existence loosens the grip the created self has on your mind, bringing to the fore your TRUE SELF.

## Remember

You started in life by fulfilling a desire and need for someone else, your parents

---

A self was created by a connection with people and objects

---

You then became an extended version with more life experience

---

It is ludicrous to believe you are a bundle of experiences, thoughts, and emotions that your mind holds onto

---

Understanding this dimension of your existence loosens the grip the created self has on your mind

# Quote

---

"We can never obtain peace in the outer world until we make peace with ourselves."
**-Dalai Lama-**

---

## Chapter Twelve:
## Your True Self

During your lifetime you've amended, adjusted, and changed beliefs about your experiences many times, some intentionally and some unintentionally. There are some moments you don't remember, but they still unconsciously affect how you think, behave, and feel. Many experiences have been exaggerated, misinterpreted, and fabricated over time. Essentially, it's all made-up substance created with thought. You can change any of the content whenever you like, decide to forget and ignore some of it, change your feelings towards it and still believe this is who you are. All of what you retain in your head is just experience, and you interpret it as "me" and "my life". They are experiences of your life, that is unquestionable, but it's not who you are.

By accumulating all these life experiences, you have confused your reality; you have created an identity in your mind by connecting millions of thoughts, emotions, and mental images to create a personality and story which you now believe is you. It's a constructed idea, a program built and made up over time. Stop and think about it for a minute: everything you have experienced since the day you were born is just an understanding through your senses, which you interpret using your mind, and this, in turn, leaves a thought and attaches an emotion. Finally, you are left with a mental image to remember it with. You now believe you are a bundle of experiences interpreted through your mind with emotions attached to them, that is it, and you limit yourself and undermine your greatness by calling it "me". If I ask you to switch yourself off from this illusion, you will find it almost impossible to do. You have become so accustomed to relating with the character your mind created, and the hardest part is, you will try to do this with the same created self that doesn't want you to. It is a paradox and predicament that you've trapped yourself in.

The good news is, you can make the shift with a level of awareness. The first step is to have the understanding that the self you have created in your mind is not who you are. Then you put in the effort to hold this awareness. It will require patience and perseverance on your part for your true self to transpire. The created self you are operating through will not co-operate and will do whatever it takes to keep you from knowing the truth. As such, there is no point in trying to convince it otherwise. You must pay attention to your thoughts. It is this exercise that will begin the process. Thought awareness implies not attaching and identifying with the thoughts but merely witnessing them. Thoughts run through your mind constantly. They don't stop, and even when you are asleep, they are active. It's all the recorded data from your life's past experiences and the illusion that is the future going around and around in your head.

It is almost impossible to stop them. However, you can become conscious of them. This awareness of thought over time removes the attachment to the created self, and you begin to have moments and feelings from a higher consciousness that are not connected to this self-image. It is that simple. However, it requires an alert attention to watch the thoughts and emotions as they happen. By doing this, you will stop interpreting them. You will start to separate yourself from these thoughts. At the moment, you see them as who you are, but in time they will become detached, and the dreamlike state will begin to fade. You will begin to notice the created self as a separate entity, the thoughts it lives through and the emotions it holds onto for its survival. As the true self begins to emerge, you automatically become more present, living for the moment becomes much easier, and this moves you into the next phase where the only moment that exists is all you perceive.

Each moment will offer a completely different significance. No longer will it be "me" and "my life", it will now be an experience of life from a higher consciousness. I can't emphasize enough in words alone how wonderful this is to know and feel. At present, all of your experiences are analyzed and examined by what they meant and how they affect you and because of this, the true value of experience is lost. Once you get a glimpse of your true self, you move from the life of want, need, can't do without, to a life that flows through you instead of against you. The true self is the part of you that has no fears, doesn't get angry, and doesn't suffer from uncertainty. It is compassionate towards other people, accepts each moment as it is, and lives life as it was meant to be.

Your true self doesn't need a name or a title, it's not interested in being better than others, it doesn't need building up, it doesn't need to rely on a past or a future, it doesn't want to judge anyone or anything, and it doesn't require fear to motivate it. It has the power to do anything; nothing is impossible. What you have created using your mind is concealing this power. To connect to the true self doesn't require a miracle or years of dedication to any concept. You need to understand that the created self is NOT who you are, and the shift is automatic. Gradually, with this awareness, you wake up and become more conscious of the self that is real and the fake self is seen for the first time for what it is.

All of your choices, decisions, actions, and reactions are through this imagined personality you relate to, which makes life challenging. Once you know this truth about yourself, life becomes more meaningful. The true self will guide you throughout and make the right choices and decisions since it will no longer have the created self getting in the way. Moving forward, you now have an option to either continue as you are or let this truth lead you to a life of fulfillment and happiness. Free will has been given to you to exercise your freedom from the created self and know the truth about who you are. For some of us, this truth is closer to understanding, but it is within reach of us all. You need to make the conscious choice.

You have the ability to learn and develop this understanding while still being predominantly under the control of the dominant force of the created self. Everyday influences in the world can make this a challenge, but once you are fully committed to practice the development of knowing your true self, despite all of the difficulties you face, the shift is only a matter of time. I've always known consciously that I'm playing out lots of different roles and never lost myself in them. At first, I didn't feel any different to anyone else. I thought the feelings and this understanding were normal for everyone until I realized that others didn't feel and think the way I did. I'm not any better than anyone else, the only difference between you and me is that the many layers of thought, experience, and memories have been dispelled and I have connected to the true self that is permanent. When I have thoughts, experiences, and memories, or feel emotions, I'm merely a witness to the created self, which is a temporary form of the mind.

With some conscious awareness on your part, this is possible for you too. Remember, it's your mind that created you; this is not preordained, or something you were born with. It is the lie a majority of humans unfortunately live with. They haven't been able to see beyond their creation and in return struggle through life and never reach a state of true, blissful living. Knowing this truth, you can live an amazing life and be happy irrespective of what is happening to you and around you.

You are already perfect, and therefore, you do not require developing, fixing, or changing. You need to be in touch with your true self. Not willing to understand the truth is ignorance. By embracing the truth you will remove the veil of ignorance and denial. You learn about yourself and the reality that lies behind what you've been conned into believing. You are free to express what you want to believe, but remember that by remaining in the dark, you are producing your reality and condemning who you truly are. I cannot underestimate the value of what I am sharing with you: to continue in the present state, you deny yourself the true meaning of your life. Living through your created self is out of alignment with everything that you are.

Instead of being in control, you have complicated your life. You have blindly trusted and believed that you are made up of your life experiences, thoughts, and actions; you have been brainwashed into thinking you are merely a bundle of memories, made up of past experiences and conditioning. You have come to accept this as your reality and are suppressed by your creation. You must align yourself with the truth and take back control of your life. Stop trying to define who you are by projecting a future, which in essence is just an illusion. Be more present, watch and witness the thoughts, and you will automatically become who you are. You will move to the higher self and remove yourself from this mind's version that isn't real, and however much you try, it will never be. This created self is not what you need, and your true self is not something you need to find. Just let go of this burden of the fake self and it will reveal itself to you. To overturn this mad reality, you must remove this false sense of security about who you are. By continuing in this thought system you deny the freedom you most desire. Remember, you are not sacrificing anything; instead, you are receiving everything. Stop limiting yourself to this ideal that has been produced by your mind and the confusion of your reality will be gone forever.

In you, the world has received an amazing gift. Human life is a rare opportunity, something you must cherish, and you need to make the most of the time you have, to live every moment, to find your real life purpose. If you want to be at peace and fulfilled in life, you need to be willing to do everything necessary and to look past what you think you know about yourself and your life. Don't stay trapped in the personality you can't see beyond. The roles you are acting out daily are holding you captive, and you have become a prisoner of your own mind's creation. We all have a deep longing to be more than just the roles we have to play out. You may believe you have been doing all the right things, being a good person, having high ethics, acting only with the best intentions, but you are at the mercy of what you have created to survive.

The realization of this transient nature will create an opening that will change everything for you. Bringing the true self out from behind the mask of the created version is the only achievement in life that is worthwhile. It is real knowledge and wisdom that gives rise to the experience of life and everything you do. Each experience will begin to come from somewhere much deeper. I can assure you that you will continue to survive without these fictional roles, and you will begin to experience a life that no role could ever offer you. You created all of these roles. Therefore, you too can dispel them by withdrawing your thoughts on them. The created self tricks you into believing it works in your best interest and is there to support your every need to make you feel better. It is the insane nature of the mind's own creation, and its primary purpose is to hold you down into believing there is no other way. The habits of your internal voice are so ingrained that even when you question its beliefs and values, it will tell you that you're ridiculous to doubt its reality. These mind tendencies cannot be fought against, and you cannot overcome it by trying to contest it against itself. You need to stay aware of its workings, and this will bring into play a higher level of consciousness and weaken the created self's grip on you. In doing so, you can awaken the true side and start living a life worth loving.

# Remember

The first step is to have the understanding that the self you have created in your mind is not who you are

---

Thought awareness implies not attaching and identifying with the thoughts but merely witnessing them

---

As the true self begins to emerge, you automatically become more present

---

Living through your created self is out of alignment with everything that you are

---

You can awaken the true side and start living a life worth loving.

# Quote

---

Be kind, for everyone you meet is fighting a harder battle.
**-Plato-**

---

## Chapter Thirteen:
## Become the Silent Witness

The development of the true self is only apparent when we become witnesses to the created self. You don't have to be confrontational to the created self or start building a struggle between the two, you merely need to be the silent witness, and the process will begin. The separation from the true self is only present because you can't see it and the created self doesn't want to believe it. There is a belligerent attitude towards the challenge the created self faces when this is brought to its attention. It is why I state that you must be ready and want to know this truth; otherwise, the created self will find reasons and objections to deny the truth.

To silence the created self requires a level of acceptance about your self-perception, without leaving the created self in a state of confusion. It is easily done if one doesn't want to accept there is anything else other than what the mind has created. At present, your identification with the created self is totally beyond question, and it is the created self that will fight and by force try to keep you away from knowing any different. You must practice with awareness to dissociate your mind from what it has created. The created self only wants to understand and believe in its creation, it cannot be controlled by more thinking whilst you are in its control. You only need to recognize it and in doing so it will begin to separate itself. It does not understand the mind; therefore, it cannot understand the truth. It is just part of your imagination.

Remember that the mind under the control of the created self can never adequately remove any self-doubt. Every time you use your mind under the power of the created self, the mind will defend its position, and it will manipulate and distort the truth, hence it is no use trying to convince it otherwise. You simply need to be conscious of it and it will begin to lose its power over you.

The created self finds it challenging to focus consistently on anything for too long. So much is happening in life, it can only absorb so much at any one time, and this makes the created self very selective in what it wants to understand. It deletes most of what is happening in the present moment and only pays attention to the thoughts, focusing on what could make it feel more significant in the future, rather than what is happening now. Anything real but insignificant to its future needs doesn't get a look in. You miss so much moment to moment and very rarely appreciate what is of real value because you are so wrapped up in what the created self needs to survive, always being deceived of what is precious at the expense of what is a temporary concept designed by your mind.

Before you can transcend this, you must understand that its sole survival is dependent on denying this truth, and it will do whatever it takes to keep you away and prevent you from revealing the truth. If you lose the early battle and continue to believe in the created self, you will remain on the road of confusion and destruction. For you to win the war against this enemy, you must understand that you have to look deeper than the created self, and the first step is to be the silent witness to the voice inside your head, to have an awareness of duality; you will begin the reversal process from created self to the true self. Once you get a glimpse of this reality, the most magnificent of feelings start, and let me assure you, it keeps getting better. As you progress through the phases of moving away from the created self, you will initially become more aware of the developing number of characteristics that have to lead you to a variety of different roles being played out. You become less confused about your life, and the mind quietens down. You will also begin to notice your thoughts, emotions, and actions more clearly while the higher true self begins to move up. The authenticity of who you are begins to emerge and removes all doubt that holding on to this created self has any long-term benefit.

When you become more conscious of your true nature, you automatically also become more present. Subsequently, the created self that likes to live in the past and future loses its energy. The most vital action on your part to understanding your true self is to become the witness of the created self by watching and monitoring your thoughts. It doesn't mean you start thinking about thinking and analyzing your thoughts; this will only add fuel to the fire. You are just to observe your thoughts in a subtle way. There is nothing here that is complicated. Be the silent witness to them. Do not associate yourself with them, and don't make them yours. Instead, understand that they are only a part of your past conditioning from experiences and of future illusions.

The created self has been your life to date. It is here where you have become familiar and comfortable. The created self has to feel unique and special for its survival. This is the basis it is formed on. Its main objective is the ongoing need to create a problem and to have the satisfaction of solving it. It is its self-fulfilling prophecy. Since it is all you have known, you need to be vigilant and stand guard against its tricks of deceiving you into believing in its ways. Constant daily focus with present moment awareness will be required. Everyday contact with the world, circumstances, and situations in your life will unintentionally keep pulling you back to the created self. Every time this happens, you have to stop and remind yourself that this is not who you are and bring yourself back into the present moment of merely being a witness to what is happening and not get drawn in.

Nevertheless, in the early stages, you have to be aware of this possibility and accept that your mind may try to confuse you and make it difficult. Also, in the beginning, you must not let any outside influences persuade you to divert from knowing this truth. Sometimes, the people closest to you may feel uncomfortable seeing this change in you, and they may feel threatened by it at first, but rest assured over time they will be amazed at your transformation, and the truth will start to influence them too.

Remember, this is a process to become the silent witness, but let me assure you, it's the only thing you can do in this lifetime that will ever be worth achieving. It is your life's purpose to understand who you are. There are no ceremonies or rituals to follow, it is a simple means of going beyond thought, not analyzing or ignoring them, just being aware, and over time the true self appears. It is not a mind-created concept. It cannot be perceived or judged with the created self; in fact, it is the created self that is getting in the way of you knowing your true self. The created self has become the mind, thus blocking the view. It doesn't require any miracles, just pure thought awareness. Once you make some initial progress, the mind under the spell of the created self will no longer be under attack and in danger. Instead, under the influence of your true self, it becomes your sanctuary. I cannot underestimate how critical it is to connect to your true self.

Without this conscious thought awareness, life will have been nothing but a futile exercise of experiences interpreted through a lie. Even though the created self can't and doesn't want to recognize this, once a connection is made, the created self will no longer be able to conceal this truth since the true self is much stronger. Your true self works in harmony with everything that is presented and accepts all that is before it as perfect, whereas the created self works to find conflict and issues in everything that is presented before it. Unfortunately, because humans only see the created version as true, through time, this is all they know and understand, and the true self is open to question.

Through the created self, your existence has become confounded, and this is because of the duality; it is always there, but you aren't conscious of it. With awareness of thought, in the end, the created self will begin to identify with itself for being superficial. The created self becomes limited to what it has to offer and is recognized for being just a role. As you begin to understand the transient nature of what you believe about yourself, it will become crystal clear. You start to notice your perception of everything changing. Prior to you understanding this truth, everything was perceived through your created self, your thoughts, emotions, beliefs, and values, even your communication with the people in your life, your understanding of them and the world around you in general. The feelings of gratitude will open you to your real self. You will also begin to appreciate the challenges and predicaments that other humans face.

Once you see the truth, you will exhibit empathy and sympathy for other humans. You will lose resentment, frustration, and anger when confronted with situations and issues involving other people. You will also begin to notice the confused state people are living through, and you will stop perceiving them through their created versions. Your presence will have a positive impact on everyone you have contact with. You will know all you need to know. You won't need your memories to feel good. Your past will be past experiences. You will, for the first time, feel complete. There will be no more questions, and old emotions will mean nothing but a conditioned response to an experience. Your thoughts will come from a higher consciousness. You will also stop living with concepts, searching for evidence and proof of the missing answers to your existence. You will have no more questions about who you are.

Every experience, emotion, reaction, and action will come from a different place. Your attachments to possessions will no longer be as strong as they were before. You can still enjoy what these things bring into your life, but they will no longer have a hold on you, and when you have to return or lose them, it will not affect you. Your standards increase because you value everything from a different perspective. You automatically become a better person. The created self was selfish, and most of its motives were for its benefit and self-image, whereas the true self has no personal needs to boost itself. Being your true self removes the pressure from always having to do something and to prove your value. It takes away the uncertainty that humans fear so much. The future is seen for the first time for what it is: an illusion. Even death will be another experience and the fear that surrounds it will dissipate.

Your mind will settle down and from now on life will be an amazing moment-to-moment experience. The true essence of living is to be happy in the present moment, and you can make that happen now by just making a connection with your true self. Living in the present moment eliminates the fears of what the future may hold, it creates an energy and vibrancy to give more to everything you set out to achieve, and you become a more deserving self. Every moment becomes special and is cherished, thus creating positive thoughts and an environment that is conducive to achieving anything you like much quicker and easier. The true self is your natural state. It is not something you acquire or search for, because you already have it. You need to have a higher standard for yourself and not accept this mind-limited version. You need to make a decision in your life to commit to knowing the truth about yourself. Don't you deserve to be happy and to lead a fulfilling life?

The created self cannot distinguish between what is the true self and what the mind had created. You have been under its enchantment for too long, but now you can finally say goodbye to the created self and prevent it from living and surviving through you. End your suffering now, stop living in your mind's creation, open yourself up, and begin the journey of being who you truly are. You can start to do this by being the silent witness to your thoughts.

# Remember

The separation from the true self is only present because the created self doesn't want to believe it

---

The mind under the control of the created self can never adequately remove any self-doubt

---

Before you can transcend this, you must understand that its sole survival is dependent on denying this truth

---

Once you get a glimpse of this reality, the most magnificent of feelings start

---

It's the only thing you can do in this lifetime that will ever be worth achieving

# Quote

———————

"There is nothing in life to fear, except your mind."
-Rany Athwall-

———————

## Chapter Fourteen:
## Humanity Is One

Every relationship you've ever had, from the moment you were born, has been judged on what you know and believe about each individual. It includes your parents and guardians, your siblings, other relatives, and friends. During your lifetime, there have also been many other people you've admired, aspired to be like, and wanted to emulate. This includes celebrities from television, the film industry, the music world, sportsmen and women, business people, and famous people throughout history, all of whom have played a role and influenced you in some capacity or another.

Everyone deserves appreciation for what they do and how they contribute to your life and the lives of others; you should never judge anyone based on their beliefs and values. Instead, you should respect them and reward them with your attention. But isn't it surprising how little value humans give each other or at times how very little they appreciate the people around them? Is this because many humans have the belief that it is people that are the cause of their problems, and it is they that get in the way of what they want? On the whole, people in the world are decent; humans want to be liked and respected. However, humans find this so difficult to do. Is it because they can only like and respect people who meet this need in them and they are always looking for the effort on someone else's part first?

To earn the respect and love of others, you must stop thinking from the perspective of the created self. When you do this, the true self connects with other humans with little effort. All humans beyond the mind's creation are the same and are only seen to be different because of what the mind has created through their own experiences. When you realize the naivety of the created self, you will start to connect genuinely with everyone you speak and interact with, and in return, their communication will become more honest and genuine towards you. Most humans don't know what it is like to have genuine relationships, because superficial ideals connect them. Too much effort is spent looking for and attempting to win the approval of the self-image, and the more they do this, the more disconnected they become.

The created self loves the drama of human interaction. It is one of many ways it deceives you to ensure its existence: the drama of being let down by others, anguish over being left frustrated and angry, having someone else to blame for insecurities and problems. The created self loves the uncertainty surrounding relationships. It's all a game the created self likes to play. Why do you love sitting in front of a screen so much? Humans are addicted to it. Soap operas, films, reality TV. These shows have become a considerable part of your life. You watch them, get caught up in them. You begin to relate to the characters and get upset with them. You enjoy watching people arguing and showing their disapproval of each other, seeing relationships breaking up, the hate and anger, followed by your spending hours talking about it as if it was all real. Why? Because it reflects the drama in your life. Situations on the screen always seem much worse, and this helps you to feel better about your own life. Drama sells, and writers, producers, and directors know this.

Even many sporting events have become spectacles of drama. It is no longer two people competing at the top of their sport. Instead, the event starts weeks before with hours of filming, watching them berating each other. The media coverage is crazy, but it's what today's human craves, the drama of the interaction between people.

All of the many relationships you've been through in your life have all been based on your needs and the needs of others. Think about this for a moment. There are many people you care about and love. Ask yourself this question: "Are my love and feelings for these people unconditional?" You will probably find the answer isn't a convincing yes. In essence, all of these people are fulfilling a need which makes you have strong feelings towards them, and of course it is in your interest to look after and protect these relationships. Observe how many different relationships you've had from your childhood to the present day, all of them offering various levels of need, some closer than others. Nevertheless, they were all important to you at some point in your life.

Think of someone you had a relationship with who is no longer in contact with you. You will notice it is because the need has gone, either for you or for them. It is typical of all relationships, even with more intimate ones. When relationships break up, people often say, "We didn't love each other anymore." However, the deeper underlying issue is that the other person wasn't fulfilling their needs anymore. Equally, even when there has been a betrayal of some kind, maybe in a friendship or business relationship, the deception would have been the cause for the breakup, but the need that was once there for a person now doesn't seem worth it or hold any value.

Another example is when someone forgives another person after being mistreated. This is because the need for that person outweighs any loss or hurt they may be feeling at that time from what had been done. And this is all to protect what the mind has created. In essence, you can never have any connection on a much deeper and permanent level while the meaning you have for relationships is based on the needs of the created self. Once you make the shift from the created to the true self, all relationships begin to have a different representation. They are no longer merely based on what someone can do, offer, or give you. Instead, it has a much deeper connection of what is the truth, and you see people in a different light.

Knowing your true self, you will improve your interaction with other human beings. Your true self responds to everything in the correct manner. Once you recognize the habitual nature of the created self towards other people, your thoughts and actions will change, making all of your relationships more meaningful. Up until now, the majority of your interaction with other people has been through something that isn't real and genuine. Therefore, it is no surprise many relationships haven't worked as effectively or lasted for very long. You have been managing your relationships in a total state of misperception. You have been trying to do this between two self-created versions that have had different life experiences and an understanding of what those experiences mean to them.

It is impossible to avoid conflicts and challenges when your operating software, the created self, cannot be compatible. How many times have you heard the phrase "We couldn't get on because we were two different people"? This statement makes me laugh because it is so apparent. Humans can never properly understand each other through the created version because they continue making up and changing this story about who they are and then spend most of their lives trying to protect it. When we see two people who are getting on and experiencing a strong connection, you will usually find that in each other's company they are very rarely thinking from the created self. They are unknowingly communicating from a higher self, and this makes the two people closer. The two almost become one at that moment.

A classic example is of a couple who fall in love. The early stages of total bliss and love are there because the created self isn't in the way as much. There is no judgment and more awareness of the moment. But soon, as the created self starts to become more prominent in the relationship, they quickly move on to feelings of threat and loss. Over time, conflicts begin to emerge; they now have expectations on the relationship and the moment they once enjoyed becomes only a future to protect. The couple also becomes more rigid towards the rules they create for each other to avoid being hurt, and they put less focus on the needs of the other, whereas at the beginning of the relationship, they were prepared to let some of the created version go to be more thoughtful and loving towards the partner, irrespective of their faults.

By losing the created self, you will no longer be easily offended by an unthoughtful gesture or remark. You will no longer feel unappreciated or disrespected. It will also, in turn, bring about empathy for the people around you and lead to a better understanding of them. You will no longer be in the constant struggle of trying to understand another person's reasoning and their refusal to view and accept yours. The created self keeps its identity based on the concept that it is unique and doesn't require observation or to be judged, thus keeping oneself away from having to eradicate opinions about others and that they can be wrong. Removing the created self, you will act more freely in the company of others without feeling the need to protect and preserve anything anymore. You will no longer fear being judged, mistreated, or misunderstood. Your interaction will be more present, and anyone in your company will feel comfortable because the feeling towards others will come from a higher and more profound position.

Similarly, your choice of language will change, the power of speech used properly. It is a beautiful gift; there is tremendous power in the spoken word. All of your erudite understanding is through words. Either you are listening to them or reading them. Words can inspire you, or they can destroy you. They create love between people and equally hate, to an extent where people are prepared to kill one another. The created self produces its version of the dictionary and the meaning of words from its own experiences. It carefully decides which words represent the most power to express how it feels and to share its own experiences. These words also represent what and how you want others to feel in your presence, or the intensity of a word to impact others. Words conjure up all sorts of mental images, and the created self knows how to do this to keep the story alive. Words can also change how you feel in an instance. The created self, based on its beliefs, makes up many preferred sentences and metaphors for the effect it can have on your emotional state.

The created self also knows how to get a reaction out of others by choosing the habitual language that has worked in the past to get the desired reaction. It also plays with words in its cunning and devious ways to get an outcome it needs. The created self also likes to make what it describes more interesting by increasing the passion of an experience. Instead of keeping it simple, it has to extend on the experience and intensify it with strong emotional words.

Your chosen language can comfort and make someone feel better or can inflict severe and long-lasting pain and destroy relationships. Many of life's difficulties stem from thoughtless communication. It's a lack of control you have over your created self that makes you say what you say and how you say it. Because you are always operating from the conscious level of the created self, what you say and communicate is to preserve this imagined self. With more focused thought, you can easily monitor your conversations and be more careful and considerate when you speak to anyone.

Most of your problems are due to the way you communicate with others. If you have more self-control over your chosen language, your interactions with others will improve. Even by you being more observant, some people may still behave no differently towards you. However, because you will understand their mental conditioning and since they don't know any different, you will always remain calm and logical by just handling what is in front of you. You can still stand your ground and deal with a situation with firmness, but it won't have an effect on you. The situation will be detached from you. There will also be moments when others try to test you, by picking out a perceived weakness and trying to cause you to react. This is because at first, they will be uncomfortable with this change in you. It's not who they are used to.

Operating away from the created self, you will no longer feel the need to blame them for any deliberate ways to antagonize you since you will recognize the spell of the created self they are under and know that if they knew any different they wouldn't behave this way. So, with this, you can take control of any situation by reminding yourself that this moment is not intentional and that you have accepted the outcome without any resistance to it. Accepting the situation will allow it to work itself out without the need for defending and attaching yourself to it. Equally, you stop seeing yourself through the eyes of other people's opinions and thoughts about who you are. You now have the understanding that you are just another version of who they think you are based only on their experience with you. In the past, the mind-self would react because it believed something of value for its survival had been lost.

Knowing your true self will dramatically alter your daily interactions with people. When you are under the influence of the created self, instead of the real purpose of connecting with people, you have been communicating with others to affect people and situations for your own needs. Throughout your life, your interactions have influenced how you see and view everyone without realizing the impact it would have. You have taken so much of what is said personally, and this has conditioned your responses and reactions with others. Negative statements and experiences with other people have affected you and created a reality you believe in; this is all part of the created self too.

Your life can be much easier to handle and manage once you've stepped away from this version that enjoys conflict with others. When you become conscious of the created self, interaction with others is no longer infused with an objective. Instead, your communication flows beautifully as each moment arises. You will no longer feel the pressure for adequate responses because you trust in the true self, whereas in the past, the created self often let you down and reacted indifferently, hence the need to always be thinking about how to respond to a situation well before you have to. The created self reacts to people from its conditioning through what the mind has created from past interactions with other people. The exact same experience with two different people can be the same, yet your reaction may be totally different because of the meaning and value you've attached to an individual. It demonstrates how the created self determines and defines people based on its needs from them and their worth.

Each day, you will face a myriad of obstacles that will sidetrack you from knowing your true self. You will be dealing with people who have no knowledge of who they really are, and this is why there is always the potential for conflict. There may also be questions that keep appearing from this created reality that you have about your relationships. People around you are operating from their version of themselves and their interpretation of what is true. You have no control over these outward circumstances and people, and what everyone believes about their situations is not for you to judge. It is only when you realize the truth that you understand and begin to see everything from a higher perspective and your reaction to people changes.

Over time, your true self will begin to affect them too, and this is when you begin to have a real relationship based on another level of love and not just needs. Once you are aware of your true self, you can make a difference to your life and show your loved ones and people in your life the way to true fulfillment and peace from their interaction with you. Beneath the self-made mind versions, humanity is ONE.

# Remember

Everyone deserves appreciation for what they do and
how they contribute to your life and the lives of others

---

All humans beyond the mind's creation are the same and are
only seen to be different because of what the mind has created

---

Most humans don't know what it is like to have genuine
relationships, because superficial ideals connect them

---

Once you make the shift from the created to the true self, all
relationships begin to have a different representation

---

It is only when you realize the truth that you understand
and begin to see everything from a higher perspective
and your reaction to people changes

## Quote

---

"True happiness is to enjoy the present, without anxious dependence upon the future, not to amuse ourselves with either hopes or fears but to rest satisfied with what we have, which is sufficient, for he that is so, wants nothing."
-Seneca-

---

## Chapter Fifteen:

## Let Emotions Flow

When you experience a negative emotion, similar to thought, it is important to accept it. These emotions don't need to be judged. They are merely a message from your body. Each feeling is a conditioned response of the created self. Don't resist them. The only thing you need to do is to discern whether any action is required on your part. For instance, is it telling you to take action or is it just a reaction to your imagination? Usually, if you have an emotion that arises because of what somebody has said or done which is perceived to be negative, invariably this is because the created self has been offended. Once you experience the thought, the emotion you feel isn't far behind. Let the two flow through you and don't make a connection of any kind.

There may be feelings of empathy and sympathy for the created self, but you can remain detached without being affected on a much deeper level. It is because you now have an understanding of the human condition, and realize it has nothing to do with your true self, and it is only the created self that has been affected. Also, with practice, you will be able to handle emotions much sooner without them becoming something bigger, and with true self-awareness, you will always be able to deal with the feelings without attaching yourself to them.

The created self always has to have a reason to be happy. It has set itself up with a group of conditions before it can be pleased about anything. Habitually, it has to have ideas and made-up stories for how it can feel good. It is because it has been conditioned from a young age about being rewarded when something good happens. I'm sure you can remember a time when you received a favorite treat from your parents for being well-behaved. Similarly, at school, you were only rewarded when you achieved a particular target or when you performed a specific task well. All of your life, the created self generates several formulas to feel happy, giving out instructions about what needs to happen and what needs to be done before it can feel good about itself.

The created self believes it can only be rewarded with happiness by achieving more and receiving recognition from others. The motivation comes from this desire to improve its self-worth. Most of the emotions you feel are there to protect what you believe about yourself, and this also involves negative reactions to anything you think is getting in your way and disturbing your mind. However, your true self doesn't react. It understands everything without judging or labeling the situation and by just dealing with what is happening at any given time. You need to become more attentive to your emotions by first removing the role you are playing and then dealing with what is in front of you. Ignorance towards emotions is keeping you trapped, and when you receive instructions from the created self, you will often jump to conclusions and develop unnecessary emotions and ideas about what is happening.

As long as your sense of vulnerability persists, emotions will always get the better of you and keep you engaged in the story your created self wants. You need to watch over emotions, especially the habitual few that still present the same outcome for you. The moment you have done this, you are identifying with the higher true self. The true self is not judgmental and only views the facts before making a decision. It avoids conflict with other people's opinions, removes emotion, and therefore remains calm in any situation.

Emotions under the influence of the created self can be challenging and put you in uncompromising situations. Reactions to your emotions become unpredictable and sometimes dangerous to your well-being and the safety of others. You will experience times of intense pain when certain emotions take over, and the first step is to accept the situation; acceptance takes away the "Why me?" question, which is the first question the created self likes to ask. Acceptance is a way of letting go of something you have no control over. It also allows you the freedom to move forward rather than being paralyzed with the pain of your emotions.

When you recognize what is happening, you automatically start to witness your thoughts and take control of your emotions, which will remove the suffering. All of the emotions you experience today are from your past conditioning, which isn't who you are. They are only part of the experience. Because they are unconscious and don't come with a warning, when they appear, you just need to accept them and remind yourself that they have nothing to do with who you are. They are only your body's conditioned reaction to a past event which is recorded in the unconscious part of your mind. If you do this, the emotion, just like a thought, will move on without disturbing you too much.

Watching and witnessing your emotions is also fundamental to understanding the truth about who we are. But from a practical perspective, how does one witness their emotions in a world that is continuously driven by the created self? You must persevere and continue monitoring your thoughts and your mind under the influence of the true self, which will handle the feeling with ease. It is therefore clear that the interpretation you give to any situation is dependent upon your understanding of who you want to serve. Once you adopt the approach from your true self, you become a better person with a strong belief that you can overcome any adversity. Experiencing life through your true self removes problems and challenges and replaces them with opportunities to grow and expand your understanding of what is real.

Remaining under the rule of the created version, you will be miserable even in the best of circumstances. Remember, it is not the situation that is the problem; it is the thoughts and emotions the created self likes to experience and feed off. When you have an awareness of your emotions, the true self regains control and balance without reacting and making a situation into another story. You will develop a habit of confronting the beast within that drives emotions and the drama it loves. Through your true self, by whatever state you are in, you will always remain firm against the negative thinking your emotions bring. Whenever you have an emotion, remember where it resides and operates from and you will dispel its power over you as your state shifts to your true self. The real escape comes over time once you fully realize the error of your ways. You may initially interpret this to be out of your reach and something you will never overcome, but I can assure you this can be achieved by staying resolute in your pursuit to eradicate this fake version that you so long to protect. When you do eventually have some control, negative emotions will be nothing to fear.

Thoughts and emotions are the tools the created self uses to keep you entangled in its existence, under its control. It likes to take credit for all emotions, including the positive ones. It believes it is responsible for instigating all feelings and emotions that are connected to its thoughts. Every emotion you ever feel has specific details of the created self linked to it. To experience real emotions, it has to come from your true self, where the experience and feeling are profound. What is the difference, you may ask? When you experience emotions from the created self, there is always a feeling of injury or something that has been achieved, for the continuation of its story, whereas with the true self, it is just an emotion which is a reaction to a thought; there is no need to create a story or belief surrounding the feeling. For example, happiness isn't experienced because you have acquired something to make the created self feel good. Instead, it's having the clarity of experiencing life beyond this imagined existence.

Even the feeling of fear is faced with courage beyond anything the created self can offer. Any psychological pain and suffering is accepted with gratitude at that moment without the need to make it into a story about yourself. Deploying gratitude will inspire you to develop a mindset that pushes you towards your true self and creates a peaceful environment of appreciation for anything you experience. Knowing that your true self exists is what you should be happy about and what you can be grateful for, rather than the needs of the created self, which are temporary and in the future result in making you unhappy.

Gratitude dispels negative emotions from the created self and encourages you to recognize the real self. Once you thoroughly learn how your created self is linked to your emotions, you can change your state in an instant by reconnecting to your true self. In the future, when you feel a negative emotion such as stress, anxiety, anger, or frustration, stop and remind yourself of its origin, and the emotion will lose its energy and power over you. It is that simple. Don't acknowledge it, label it, try to understand it, and don't dwell on it. As you learn to understand the truth about yourself, your mind will stop analyzing and automatically start to handle life situations and allow emotions to flow through you without any impact.

# Remember

Each feeling is a conditioned response of the
created self. Don't resist them

---

The created self believes it can only be rewarded with happiness by achieving more and receiving recognition from others

---

Emotions under the influence of the created self can be
challenging and put you in uncompromising situations

---

Acceptance allows you the freedom to move forward rather
than being paralyzed with the pain of your emotions

---

Remaining under the rule of the created version, you will
be miserable even in the best of circumstances

## Quote

---

"Wise men talk because they have something to say; fools because they have to say something."
**-Plato-**

---

## Chapter Sixteen:

## Allow Life to Happen

You live in a world which offers so much to experience and enjoy, but it is the created self who believes you can only truly feel happy and fulfilled by having events and life work out the way you want and desire. This is why so many humans live in a state of frustration and constant disappointment. I'm not suggesting you shouldn't have desires. However, it's your attitude and approach to life when things don't go the way you want that becomes the root of your problems. There is a myth or belief that life is too short and that a human must experience as much as possible before their life comes to an end. However, with this belief comes a level of expectancy that makes you unhappy.

Life is constantly changing, and change is inevitable. Nothing in anyone's life remains the same. Everything you have today will one day either change or leave you permanently. Your body is continually changing, people come and go in your life, possessions are new one day, and then they are old and of no value, work and career commitments change, and even your beliefs and values are frequently shifting. Have a look around you today and at your past and you will notice how temporary everything is. It can be a scary thought, and for some humans, it is tough to come to terms with.

The created self has a perpetual need to be in control of every situation, all potential outcomes, the people in their lives, and the future. Understanding how transient life is causes humans to feel vulnerable, subsequently losing their balance and control when going through difficult times. The world is going mad with the amount of unnecessary pressure humans put on themselves to control their lives. It's no surprise that every direction you look people are stressed, worried, and anxious about who they are and what will become of them. This fear encourages people to behave bizarrely in their desperation to feel certain about their future. Some even go in search of humans who are believed to have psychic powers, or fortune tellers and palm readers, anyone that might give them some solace to hold on to. Others may revert to the power of prayer in their attempt to prevent a perceived negative outcome or future. You cannot stop or control the inevitable and it is bordering on insanity to believe you can.

The created self lives with the illusion that it has control. Of course, there are certain aspects of control you can measure by the amount of effort and desire that has been applied, but you cannot prevent change however hard you try. Hence, it doesn't take many years of life experience for a human to concede to the fact that they cannot always remain in a state of happiness and instead decide to settle for moments of pleasure to escape from the reality they have created.

The created self believes it knows what is best for you and what you need. From the moment it wakes up in the morning, the created self gets to work asking what it is likely to be up against today, judging every situation, outcome, person, and conversation it is a part of. It is so typical of the make-up of the created self to be impulsive, to make quick judgments, and to berate others is natural and easy to do. However, to challenge itself and to think more logically, it takes effort, something the created self finds very difficult to do. Because of its desire to be right, the created self is also well renowned for making its opinion about everything known. It has a relentless nature to prove that everything it either doesn't approve of or disagrees with is wrong. Most arguments and disagreements are born from the created self's need to be right. What is the created self maintaining by being right? Is it to ensure it feels more significant and that there will always be a need for it?

The mind's version is endlessly looking for ways to make others believe in its story or be more understanding about its needs. It very often comes out of the fear of being treated as secondary or being rejected. It is the created self that likes to wallow in self-pity and waste time asking negative questions like "Why did this have to happen to me?" and "Why now?", whereas when you connect to your true self, the mind is always searching for ways to improve a situation in life without complaining and questioning it. The purpose of your mind is to solve life challenges and allow life to happen, not to create something that is always in need and can never be satisfied. The happiest and most successful people are not the ones who don't have any challenges, because that is impossible, but the people who know how to accept them as a part of this journey we call life.

Challenges that you have to face daily come in all sorts of shapes and sizes, but problems are always in the future, and the created self prefers to live in the future rather than dealing with what is in front of it now. It likes to spend time thinking about the problem, worrying over it, panicking, asking disempowering questions, and musing about the negative impact it may offer in the future. It is the consistent response of the mind's version to challenges in life, whereas the true self remains calm under pressure, deals only with facts, and thinks logically about the possibilities. Your true self allows the mind to do what it is meant to, to be creative and to find adequate solutions, whereas the created self enjoys making the problem a part of its identity and adding to its own story.

The created self creates needs and desires based on what it feels is required and in line with what makes it feel good. These wants are like two hands around your neck, shaking you into submission to ensure everything continues to flow as you wish. As mentioned earlier in the book, the mind creates a role in advance of what a particular need or desire will portray once attained; the need or desire by itself is never important. It is always about what value it can add to the created self. Think about this. Even when you do achieve something you wanted and that made you feel good at that moment, the mind, at some near point in the future, will decide the actual need isn't of much value anymore, that it was only about enhancing the self-image, which in turn becomes a burden because it now needs looking after. It is a vicious circle and is typical of the human state.

The goals and desires your mind settles on is not what makes you happy in the end, it's always about the self-image and approval of others, and this is what the created self thrives upon. Humans are always protecting created self-image, that's why they never enjoy anything they attain for very long. The mind quickly moves to the preservation of the self-image and the roles being played out. The goal it thought would make it happy is quickly forgotten about. Humans keep setting themselves up for disappointment; there is too much thought and effort spent on defining what they want from life and what will make them feel content, happy, and fulfilled. Unfortunately, even after many years of practice and due diligence, they never figure out why this isn't possible. The problem is that you cannot be in control while you're under the influence of what you have created with your mind. This version of you wants to stay in control and has confused you into believing this is what you need.

The created self loves this dilemma because it helps to stay in the game. Therefore, even when it is suffering, it is achieving its ultimate goal, the continuation of its survival. We have to practice asking the question of what we want or believe we need, and of how much of it is for our self-image. There may be the suggestion in your mind that an element of it may induce the self-image and this is fine to some degree. However, when it is solely for the purpose of adding to this created self, you will have a problem in the future.

Once you begin to lose the created self, instead of wanting life to be a certain way, you will start to allow life to happen for you. Uncertainty doesn't bring about negative emotions anymore. Instead, uncertainty becomes exciting, and this allows life to be experienced through you. The "Why me?" question, which can often lead to more pain when something goes wrong, is removed and replaced with acceptance. You begin to let go of something you have no control over. It also allows you the freedom of moving forward rather than being paralyzed with pain. It is inevitable that all humans will experience periods of suffering during their lifetimes. This may be a substantial financial loss, being involved in an accident, being diagnosed with a serious illness, or worse still, the death of a loved one, but who suffers? It is the conditioning response of the created self that feels it has lost something and therefore finds it difficult to accept. I'm not suggesting that these moments should be easy to deal with, but the level of suffering can be reduced immensely by knowing the truth about your reality.

You have an inner resolve and strength to deal with anything thrown your way. It is the created self that tries to obscure this from you to remain in power. All humans go through situations in their lives when they believe they can't cope and, to their surprise, they somehow find the strength, resolve, and fight they never thought they had. It isn't the created self that does this. It is your true self that emerges because you are not conscious of it. The true self goes unnoticed. You may have already experienced brief moments in your life of deeper phases of happiness and contentment during difficult times. Unconsciously, it's because you detached yourself from the created self, and this made you feel better. Unfortunately, because you can't discern from the created self, you never connect fully with who you really are. You need to be more conscious of it, and you too will begin to see your true self more often through these tough times and all other experiences. Can you imagine a life where you can still enjoy everything that the world has to offer, but you don't fear losing any of it? This would feel amazing, knowing that you are not reliant on anything to be happy and that you sit in a place where blissful living and peace already reside.

It can only be realized by knowing your true self and without setting rules and requirements to be happy. Then everything becomes an experience without questioning the outcome or the need to label it. Being connected to your true self removes the personality behind the needs and wants and gives everything you aspire to achieve a more significant meaning, because you allow life to happen through you rather than trying to control it.

# Remember

Everything you have today will one day either change
or leave you permanently

---

The created self lives with the illusion that it has control

---

Once you begin to lose the created self, instead of wanting life
to be a certain way, you will start to allow life to happen for you

---

Imagine a life where you can still enjoy everything that the
world has to offer, but you don't fear losing any of it

---

Uncertainty doesn't bring about negative emotions
anymore. Instead, uncertainty becomes exciting, and
this allows life to be experienced through you

# Quote

---

'Be content with what you have; rejoice in the way things are. When you realize there is nothing lacking, the whole world belongs to you.'
-Lao Tzu-

---

# Chapter Seventeen:
# Stop Limiting Your Greatness

Many of the beliefs you inherited were from your parents and guardians. This later extended into what you were taught in the classroom. As you got older, you started to connect to the wider world. With this, your beliefs continued to expand and change with age. The created self needs to form its opinion to be unique and has limited your experiences from its perspective. This, in return, has controlled and restricted what you believe you are capable of. I'm not suggesting you should discard your beliefs. These are very important to a human being for them to have an understanding and some direction in their life. The challenge is when they are only to fulfill the needs of the created self. This makes them weak and of no real value.

Throughout your life, you have also adopted a number of values, things that are more important to you; these values sit on top of every choice and decision you've been making. Unfortunately, it is the created self that has decided what these values are. Like needs, they are only necessary until they lose their appeal. You must keep these values in perspective. They only define what your created self believes is important, and this shadows and prevents you from searching for the truth about who you are and what is possible for you. The created self likes to place conditions on you, so it can hold you down to several beliefs and values that keep it in control, therefore making you believe it is the real motivation behind what you want. How do you define yourself today? Do you have a primary thought or belief about yourself? For example, are you a kind and generous person, someone everyone likes, or are you a strong character that people admire? Does the job that you do for a living define who you are? Are you a doctor, a lawyer, or a teacher even, or would you describe yourself as a successful person, or someone powerful and wealthy? Maybe you see yourself from a negative perspective. Are you a depressed person, an unlucky individual, or are you a victim of life? Of course, the answer to this question is made up of lots of ideas and beliefs, but all examples are only part of the imagined mind-created self.

You have also been taught from a young age to voice your opinions, and about the importance of having a strong personality to protect the identity your mind has created. You have the belief that respect and recognition can only be achieved by displaying a strength of character and demonstrating who you are and what you stand for. The created self's beliefs and values can be so conflicting, it can make you believe you have to be rich to be successful and at the same time make you believe money is the root of all evil and having too much money can lead to more problems.

Another typical example is it can make you think you need to appreciate and respect others and, at the same time, believe people are the cause of your problems. These are just some instances of how the created self has clouded your mind and left you fighting internal battles unknowingly. This is the foundation of what you are using to function in this world: a product your mind has created that is contradictory and inconsistent. These types of conflicting messages are installed by the mind when creating the self-image, which is now all hardwired into you. It's no surprise you are so confused and frustrated about how you feel most of the time.

Working from the level of the created self, humans only have access to a malfunctioning mind that has been damaged with thought. However, getting in touch with your true self automatically removes old patterns of beliefs and values held by the created self. When the true self emerges, the old beliefs and values don't come into the equation. Instead, they become congruent with your true self. And as you gain knowledge and an understanding of the truth, you begin to realize how much previous beliefs and values of the created self were impacting your life.

Knowing your true self does not demotivate you from the desire to have a great life. You will still have goals in your life. In fact, you become more inspired to do whatever is possible for you with perseverance and with the freedom that comes without the fear of failing. Once you make that connection, you will no longer be phased or question any outcome if it is different to what was planned. Having confidence and self-belief is short-lived while its home is at the feet of the created self. When something goes wrong, the created self inevitably falls apart and loses control. It is because nothing is permanent or lasts for very long when you function through the mind-created self. Also, every time a situation arises that you didn't expect or want, the created self has to find ways to pick itself up and start again. This becomes a vicious circle of building self-confidence only for it to break again.

An example of this is when a person believes they've accomplished something of value and feels elated in that moment, only to find themselves feeling despondent and dejected soon after because of some perceived setback or failure. It creates a pattern in you between desire and disappointment of when you want something that you believe will make you happy but also fear not getting what you want because you don't want to feel bad, another trick of the created self to keep you entangled in thought. Most humans are in conflict with this throughout their lives, this fear of wanting something but not risking the need in case they can't handle the disappointment. They say one thing and do another, and there is always a disparity between what they would like to happen and what they fear most.

All humans have dreams, desires, and want to lead more comfortable lives, and there is absolutely nothing wrong with that. However, it is the thought of failing in their pursuit and losing their self-image which fills them with fear to the extent of not even wanting to try that becomes the problem. You must break free from the fear of not getting what you want. Setbacks are inevitable, and they are just another outcome and experience of the created self's perception of what something means. The reason the created self reacts to situations this way is because it can't ever remain consistent and genuine towards any beliefs and feelings permanently; this is its conditioning.

The created self succumbs to negative thoughts and is always looking for excuses for why it isn't possible when something goes wrong to protect its self-worth. The only way you can have permanent self-belief irrespective of what happens in your life is when you realize your true self, the energy and positivity that is produced from your true self, is much stronger and completely different. Your true self-worth is with you forever, and it cannot ever be affected by outside circumstances and beliefs. Connecting to your true self, you have a state of mind that is capable of anything, and any self-doubt will become a thing of the past. My life has been an amazing journey. There have been many ups, and as with everyone a few downs, but amongst everything that has happened to and with me, there has lived a sensation, a feeling of being a witness to it all. It hasn't always been prevalent because of the lack of awareness in me. It was for many years camouflaged with my belief of who I was. This created a self-image I believed and trusted in. For many years now, my awareness has opened this door wider and allowed me to view the experience of life from a higher perspective, a place where I feel blessed just for the experience, irrespective of what life throws at me. I can still have moments where I'm drawn into this drama of life and lose myself in it, but these moments are very fleeting and brief. It isn't long before I'm back into the place of just being. I have more presence and appreciation of what the world and life offers, and each moment is viewed as a gift. Everyone in my life means so much more than merely a relationship fulfilling a need and their version of who they believe they are. Understanding the truth requires your full attention and when this is realized, you will have a life full of peace and tranquility.

    The default setting given to you is by your environment, and this leads you to believe you are what the mind has created and the roles you are acting out. This belief is guarding you against your true self. Your own mind's creation is the source of all your problems and is preventing you from putting an end to the misery it causes. Don't hold on to these limiting beliefs and values of who you are and what is possible for you. Be courageous, and connect to the truth to start living an extraordinary life. With thought awareness, you will discover your true identity and remove the limiting beliefs and values of the created self.

## Remember

It is the created self that has decided what these values are.
Like needs, they are only necessary until they lose their appeal

---

The created self's beliefs and values can be so conflicting

---

Getting in touch with your true self automatically removes old
patterns of beliefs and values held by the created self

---

Once you make that connection, you will no longer be phased
or question any outcome if it is different to what was planned

---

With thought awareness, you will discover your true
identity and remove the limiting beliefs
and values of the created self

# Quote

---

"We must not lose faith in humanity. Humanity is an ocean, if a few drops of the ocean are dirty, the ocean does not become dirty."
**-Mahatma Gandhi-**

---

# Chapter Eighteen:
# Your Natural State

In each phase of your life, you are essentially experiencing a level of mental well-being, and this affects your behavior, thoughts, and emotions. Mental health issues and other mind-related disorders are pervasive; people of all ages are suffering, and there are so many contributing factors that make these conditions difficult to manage and overcome. However, being emotionally and mentally healthy is more than being free of psychological issues. It requires a deeper understanding of how the created self works and about the power that has been handed over to fully appreciate why so many people are suffering from these issues. There is so much talk today in the media about mental problems, and how modern life is the source. Humans are having to deal with so much more on a daily basis and are exposed to so much threat. The created self is having to defend itself from so many angles and continuously feels like it is on the receiving end. The daily fight is exhausting, and humans are losing their resolve.

There is the burden of the past that is carried through time. The present is often frustrating, and the future is always so uncertain; what should one do? Your mind has designed a self and a life that needs a huge amount of your time and attention. There is so much to do and achieve on a daily basis. If it's not your personal needs, it is usually the needs of your loved ones. These people in your life are of course important to you, and you don't want to let anyone down, but the demands are sometimes so excessive that it causes you to worry if you believe you aren't doing enough to fulfill your responsibility towards their needs. Then you have your work and career commitments, the schedules day after day, the targets, meeting after meeting; it's a never-ending cycle. Is it any surprise you feel negative most of the time? I'm familiar with some working environments where there is a belief that stress and mental pressure are needed for employees to perform at expected levels. The manipulation and demands on humans in the workplace are massive, and whether you are working up the ladder or controlling things from above, humans have become victims of their own and other people's desires and needs. Unfortunately, until you begin to understand that your life is more than meeting deadlines and the expectations of everyone around you, you can never be happy and free from stress and worry.

More serious conditions such as depression are born from a troubled mindset of negative thought patterns built over time. A depressed state arises from a sense of loss or of being deprived of something you desperately want or believe you need. Depression covers a number of strong emotions. Feelings of frustration, of being anxious, worried, feeling guilty, and even boredom can be a catalyst for depression. Questions such as "Why do I feel depressed?" or "Why am I always so anxious?" are all too common from the created self, and there is always an unconscious benefit hidden behind the feeling.

Mental issues have become a common excuse for the human. Every time someone feels a little overwhelmed, it is all down to the pressures of life, and humans love to play the victim. It is almost like some humans enjoy this attention of being mentally unstable. Today, every negative feeling or situation requires a name and a solution to solve it, whether it is a method, a design to implement a program for the sufferer, or a drug that has been developed by a company to make a profit from the symptoms. It is all manufactured for one purpose, to persuade the human that they have a problem. I'm not suggesting that humans don't have mental issues caused by their problems` and lifestyle, but does everything need to be broken down into small parts and labeled so the individual can attach themselves to it and create another identity by the suffering it causes? By highlighting these mental diseases, the created self reinforces the story behind its made-up reality. Being stressed and depressed is unconsciously making people believe they need to be miserable to remain consistent. The unfortunate part is it also prevents humans from searching for a more meaningful answer as to why the human mind has become so destructive.

Any habitual negative mind patterns have a profound effect on the hold the created self has over you. The conditioned mind creates habits to fill voids and insecurities about who you are, and it makes you believe you are reliant on these behaviors and thoughts. We live in an age of ulcers and nervous breakdowns; most people are living with a constant fear of what may be. These negative feelings affect the decisions and choices you make, which in return gives you the results you are trying to avoid. It is a vicious circle and one you need to keep away from at all costs. Negative feelings become habitual in a concise period. They drain your energy and make you believe all sorts of nonsense. When you focus on negative situations and outcomes, your thoughts become clouded and you can very easily lose control.

As soon as you begin to understand your created self, you will realize it's just a decision you need to make with conviction and practice until it is a habit. It's merely shifting to a belief that by holding on to your habitual thoughts and feelings you are putting in a request to make the situation or outcome much worse. The all-important decision is to choose between the motives of the created self that lead to pain and misery or the purpose of the true self, which leads to something that will bring peace and happiness into your life. All decisions and choices have consequences; hence, you cannot afford to be complacent when it comes to identifying with the created self. It is a well-known fact that external circumstances and conditions are subject to change and are not in your control. You only have control over what something means to you and how you react to it. Of course, some decisions and choices are more challenging to make, and this is only because of your present state of mind.

The secret is to remain focused and give the necessary time to stay awake to the manipulative strategy of the created self. This attention should not be compromised at any time of your life, no matter how difficult life may seem. Equally, you shouldn't become frustrated with yourself at any point if some of the decisions and choices you need to make seem challenging. Knowing your true self is a process. Patience is required, and over time it will become much easier. As you get closer to your natural state of peace and happiness, the question of right or wrong choices doesn't even arise because you are now operating from a higher consciousness.

The key to a peaceful and happy life lies in the effort you make to eliminate the negative tendencies of the created self and take the road back to your natural state. The character traits that we all should be conscious of attaining, such as kindness, humility, and honesty, are all part of the true self. However, the created self believes they exist because of its own efforts and that it deserves recognition for them. When you begin to become conscious of the mind-self, you will notice the created self looking for approval for its good behavior. It is going to be an ongoing process to recognize the habitual nature of the created self and its clever tricks, an arduous one without doubt, but one that is imperative for anyone who wishes to be happy and live a life of freedom. By witnessing your habitual nature, you learn to achieve some control and expand your consciousness. You also start to understand the lack of awareness you have about your true self and how it has impacted your natural state.

What the created self desires is at the essential part of your habitual thoughts and actions, the driving force behind what motivates you to please and satisfy its needs to be happy. This feeling only lasts for a short time until the novelty wears off and you then set another target for being happy, and postpone being happy until that wish has come true. The cycle goes on and on. However, this would be a great concept to use and follow if everything you desired and wished for came true, but you know that doesn't happen, so the inevitable result of not getting what you want causes you to feel unhappy, frustrated, bored, angry, and many of the other negative emotions you want to avoid. Everywhere you look, most of the damage is created from people who have developed a habitual nature to feel negative. They don't know how to break out of this cycle, and some even believe changing would bring about more pain.

My connection to the true self has enabled me to remove all self-defeating habitual thought patterns. Instead of having thoughts that were controlling me, I'm now at a place where life is a gift, moment to moment, and I can easily accept change without the fear of loss. You too can easily change or stop any unwanted habits and behaviors controlling you without feeling you are personally sacrificing anything. You have so much around you that you miss every day because of your habitual nature of living life through your created self. You don't see the true miracle of life. Instead, you look through these tinted spectacles that have masked the glory of being and witnessing this magical world and energy that life has to offer.

As you begin living away from the habits of the created self, problems and challenges are accepted for what they are, and instead of wishing things were different, you move into a space where you deal with what is in front of you without losing your balance. It is the created version of you which feels insecure and uncertain when faced with problems, out of fear of what may happen to it, and this adds to the negative experience by rejecting what it is.

It is self-evident and needs no authentication that everyone wants to be at peace, whether you are aware of it or not. The natural state of the human is contentment and peace, however the habitual state is when the created self decides to have thoughts and feelings that bring about negative thoughts and emotions. When there is unrest and resentment, in that moment you should allow the feeling to be. Do not resist it and at the same time do not give it any attention. Eventually, your mind will realize this and move on. Your created self will always be looking for reasons to have a particular feeling if there is a hidden need beneath it.

The created self doesn't have a feeling for no reason. You may not always understand at the time why you may be feeling off or a bit low, but from the conditioned program you are operating from, the created self always unconsciously knows why. It's just about making a decision with conviction and practicing until it is your habit not to entertain these thoughts about being stressed and worried. You need to make a conscious effort by shifting your thoughts to the higher self that knows this is all the doing of the created self and a way of keeping you trapped. Remember, when you get caught unaware, stop yourself from indulging in these thoughts and tell yourself it was just a temporary lapse about what you believe and is not your natural state. Until you discover this is not who you are and as long as you live in a world of the created self, you will always be at the mercy of your feelings, and with them the thoughts and emotions they present.

You don't have to start analyzing everything you do habitually but it's vitally important to monitor any negative behaviors or actions by first being aware of them, followed by reminding yourself it is your created self that falls prey to these weaknesses. You should question the motive every time a thought appears from the created self. This is the level of awareness that is required to connect to your real self. By doing this, you will start to notice how the created self works and begin the process to empower the real you and take back control over your life and happiness. Make the decision and choice to improve your life by witnessing your created self, which interacts with your every thought and belief about your habits. You need to use your mind wisely and use all of its power to make the necessary adjustments to understand what is holding you back from being truly at peace.

The concept of who you are comes in many forms and is created unconsciously with your mind, your attitude towards life, the consistent behavior you choose, and the emotional states you are more comfortable with. The more you habitually become the witness to your thoughts, the easier it becomes to get the ultimate control over the created self and move into the space where the awareness weakens the mind-self. This subtle practice speeds up the process towards finding your natural state and losing the habitual state.

## Remember

Being emotionally and mentally healthy is more
than being free of psychological issues

---

Your mind has designed a self and a life that needs
a huge amount of your time and attention

---

The conditioned mind creates habits to fill voids and
insecurities about who you are

---

The secret is to remain focused and give the necessary time to
stay awake to the manipulative strategy of the created self

---

This subtle practice speeds up the process towards
finding your natural state and losing the habitual state

# Quote

---

"If you are depressed you are living in the past, if you are anxious you are living in the future. If you are at peace, you are living in the present."
-Lao Tzu-

---

# Chapter Nineteen:
# Simply Amazing

At birth, we've been given an amazing body, every part of it; what an invention and miracle it is. Even with all of the abuse it suffers from us for so many years, it still has the ability to fix itself. Of course, like everything, it has its own limitations and does eventually fall prey to time and any severe attack or illness. But overall it is truly a fantastic machine, working day and night, year after year, continually keeping us alive and well. Just imagine for a minute all the different functions operating at the same time. You have your organs, the heart that pumps blood around your body, the lungs that use air for you to breathe, the liver that detoxifies chemicals, and the kidneys that maintain your fluid balance. You also have the immune system that prevents infections from invading your body and the nervous system, which consists of the sensory organs.

There is one more tool that is more amazing then all of them put together: YOUR MIND. Sadly, you have confused it by believing the content of your mind from your life experiences is who you are. Like the other organs, it is given to you as an instrument to function in this world. Instead, you have put limitations on your mind and made it dysfunctional. Rather than being the go-to place for help, it has become the cause of your problems and unhappiness. You have identified with it and personalized it as "me" when, in fact, it is the thinking machine that operates to help you solve life challenges and keep you safe. Your mind has become this way because you have attached yourself to its every thought about the experiences you have been through, the data it has picked up over the years, and the recorded interpretations from these experiences. Your mind is made up of life situations, outcomes, scenarios, and dilemmas. These have now become your conditioned beliefs of who you are. Much of the mind's identity is made up of your vague and selective memory, all interpreted depending on the environment and mindset you were in at the time. Such a powerful instrument that is now weak and has become your most significant battle; it is the cause of the negativity in your life, all the worry, the fears, the anxiety, and many other mental challenges. Furthermore, because of its nature to be addictive, it is also the cause of your health issues.

I have come to realize the inconsistent behavior of the mind under the spell of the created self, and how thoughts and memories change depending on the perspective they are viewed from. You can have the same thoughts in different circumstances and your feeling towards the experience changes, hence the created self presents random answers to whatever it decides something should mean, and this can change your past in an instance, therefore changing the belief of who you are. Your reality becomes a reflection of the original illusion. You are not an object of your experience; the present state of your mind is conning you into believing that you are made up of these experiences and thoughts. All you believe and know about yourself is in your past, events and experiences that have already happened.

You are here and now but your belief about yourself is in the past and in the illusion that is the future. When you search for a reference about who you are, you look into the past, a past that can be interpreted many ways and keeps changing with time. Its fleeting nature is keeping you away from discovering the truth. Throughout your life, you have experienced and identified so much with your mind, and it has been through so many situations, interpreting each moment for you. There have been so many development stages, all viewed and interpreted either as good or bad. Because of this, the mind has become unreliable, untrustworthy, inconsistent, changeable, forgetful, easily influenced, and no longer of any real value. The mind cannot operate to its full potential because it has been destroyed with your identification and the label you have given it.

The mind is in a confused state at the best of times. You've converted your best ally into your enemy. It is the nature of your conditioned mind to give expression to your thoughts. You truly are the architect of this created self and the life you are living. The conditioned thinking patterns that run unconsciously in your head have taken total control over you, as you keep reacting in the same way to situations in your life from your past experiences. These thoughts have to lead to actions and actions have to lead to reactions.

Once you acknowledge and understand that your personal story is only in your mind, you can now start making the shift away from the created self and accessing the real power the mind possesses. After I discovered my real self, it was clear to see how attached I was to my mind under the influence of the created self, how this had been affecting every area in my life, and the tremendous impact it had on who I thought I was. You need to use the mind beyond the limitations you have put on it. When a human is performing anything at a very high level, there is no thought or identification with the created self. This is when the mind is doing the real work it was created for.

Think about a time in your life when you were at your absolute best, when you were in the moment so to speak, and you amazed yourself with the results. It could have been something you created or designed, a work of real art that you are proud of. Perhaps you made an inspiring speech in front of hundreds of people that you didn't believe you could. Maybe you exceeded your own personal best at a task or solved a problem that you couldn't see beyond— anything that made you think "Where did that come from?" or "How did I do that?" If you play any sport regularly, you will have had moments when you were entirely in the zone and on a level that is perceived to be your best. Whatever you were doing seemed to be much more comfortable, as if something more powerful had taken control. It is when you are performing beyond the created self; there is no thought from the created self, you are operating solely through the instinctive and intuitive nature of your mind, through what has been learned and mastered, not through the limitations of the created self. Imagine what it would feel like if this part of you was switched on all the time or you knew how to connect to it when needed.

Unfortunately, you have damaged this fantastic gift by creating and applying limitations to it. I cannot underestimate how much your present condition is a result of the mind losing itself in this illusion you are living through. Your mind has the ability to deal and handle anything that presents itself, and moreover has the capacity to solve any of life's challenges.

Regrettably, as I have alluded to many times, you have immobilized the mind and constrained it by believing in a fabrication that has been created through life experience. The created self is an unnecessary enemy and needs to be brought to justice. It is only interested in sustaining a temporary story that will one day inevitably end. You have a choice to either live through this imagined self and prevent the mind from functioning at the peak of its powers or make the conscious decision to eliminate the fake story and connect with your true self, empowering what is permanent and always perfect.

The personality you call "me" is just a figment of your imagination. It's no surprise you struggle through life when that is what you believe. It is insanity. You've identified so much with your mind experiences and thoughts that you've lost yourself in them, along the way destroying your most valuable asset: your mind.

# Remember

At birth, we've been given an amazing body, every part of it.
What an invention and miracle it is

---

Just imagine for a minute all the different organs
operating at the same time, keeping us alive and well

---

There is one more tool that is more amazing then all of them
put together: YOUR MIND

---

Such a powerful instrument that is now weak and has
become your most significant battle

---

You've converted your best ally into your enemy

# Quote

_____

"Knowing yourself is the beginning of all wisdom."
-Aristotle-

_____

# Chapter Twenty:
# Being Thoughtless

You have thousands of thoughts every day which stream incessantly through your mind. Although you can't stop them, you can certainly have an understanding about the essence of these thoughts and not give them the focus your created self desires. We are all born into a diversity of circumstances, and this will, for sure, influence us as to how we think and behave. But this shouldn't control what you believe about who you are. You need to go beyond these thoughts that dominate your thinking, which has automatically created an identity that is the illusion in your head.

Most of your thinking on a daily basis is absorbed by what the created self needs and how it wants to feel. Thought has its distinct values, especially when you are faced with a challenge. However, it's the habitual nature of the thought patterns you are at the mercy of that is keeping you from having peace of mind and experiencing the true essence of life. Thoughts are killing humans, and they are possessed either by pain from the past or the uncertainty of the future. The created self does not like presence, or being without thought, because without thought it cannot exist; it can only stay alive through having a past and a future. It is its sole purpose to keep you entangled in its drama and story.

It wants peace of mind and to be happy, but makes you believe this can only be achieved sometime in the future, whereas the present moment is to search for ways to have more pleasure now, to enjoy more of life. It is where the misperception lies between being happy and having moments of pleasure. Pleasure is often confused with happiness. It is the belief of the created self. It figures out ways to be free of thought by indulging in things that bring in moments of pleasure to quieten the mind like drinking alcohol, taking substances, overeating, and many other less destructive habits. These are the behaviors that determine your reality, and it's the dominating thoughts that trigger what you believe, and subsequently, this belief is acted upon. Your thoughts and actions are the cause of what is manifested into your life, and every action has some degree of influence upon what you continue to believe and trust in.

With your imagination of who you think you are, this so-called "me" feels real. You believe you know what is best for you, and the belief comes from what you have created about yourself with your thoughts. You have done this independently, and every one of us has the power to overcome it, through awareness. It is particularly important to realize the duality you face on a day-to-day basis which goes unnoticed. The thought-created you and your true self are constantly at battle, and the created self always comes out on top. Your current state is a prime example of how obvious this predicament you are in is. With the power and persistence of the created self your limited thoughts and actions of who you are come as no shock.

These cycles and patterns of thought are all from the viewpoint of the created self, and there is no necessity to know the truth while it is in control. To find the truth for yourself is first to understand the transient and ever-changing nature of your thoughts.

Deep down, we are all aware of this. The interaction between the two is very subtle, and to the unknown, this cannot be seen. However, with the awareness of thought, you begin to develop presence and start to discern between the two. Your true origin was first and has always been there. The mind-self wants to believe this, but only through thought. The created self needs the recognition of knowing the truth, when in fact it only exists with thought and therefore is not in a position to see the truth.

The created self is searching to find ways to become permanent, and survival is its number one priority. In reality, to realize the true self, you must first understand that the created self isn't real. Therefore, anything you experience through your thoughts is also not real. The created self takes advantage of all situations and loves to compliment itself on overcoming any issues of self-doubt. Overcoming self-doubt is one of its key components to ensure its survival. I'm not suggesting you should ignore this fact. However, what you should do is stay alert to its nature and be aware that it cannot affect you unless you continue to believe it to be real.

Most of a human's thoughts are negative. This is the unconscious default setting that the created self has installed and to feel good it has created a belief that it has to search for ways to feel better. This method and system is in place to remain in control. The consequence of this is that life starts to control you rather then you taking control of your life. It's not your circumstances, environment, or external events that control how you should feel. In you, there is the energy and strength to win back your true self and live a life worth living. You must act on its vibrant energy by being more aware of your feelings and thoughts when they arise.

This continual attempt to focus and understand the intrinsic nature of the created self will gain momentum and lead you towards a life of happiness and peace. As I have already alluded to in previous chapters, you have to practice thought awareness from a higher level. You need to develop the right attitude towards attaining control over the created self. Of course, initially it will feel like a struggle, but I assure you any effort will be worthwhile. The results of understanding your true self are magical. If you can recognize the thoughts that go through your mind, if you can witness your mental-emotional reactive patterns as they happen, then that dimension is already emerging in you.

As the awareness in which thoughts and emotions occur and the content of your life become transparent, you become the director of your life instead of the actor, and you can start to write the script you desire. Once you adopt the approach of not trusting your thoughts from the created self, you become more open-minded and develop a strong belief. You can overcome any challenge. You begin to see more clearly that it's not the situation or the circumstances that are the problem but the conditioned thought patterns of the created self or its deliberate tendency to have a negative attitude that is at the core of what you feel. You will become more conscious of the inner chatter that supports your journey to realizing the trap you are caught up in.

Your mind has created something which is very powerful and requires great thought awareness and presence to overcome, but once you are aware of this depressing state you are in, the journey towards the true self has started. You are the master of these thoughts, and you can't afford to ignore that your mind has created your reality at this level and should you continue, the harder it will become to lose this created self that the mind continues to work for. To get in touch and access the real you, you must only use your thoughts for what you have learned and what you need to know to survive in this world. You must stop using your thoughts to form an opinion about yourself or to create a story and call it "my life". Stop judging yourself and your past. It only exists through your mind. Once forgotten, it disappears, and with it the illusion of your created self. You cannot expect to remove yourself from the enslavement of the mind without any conscious effort. It is all about the awareness first, followed by conscious action on your part. By doing this, you will move into a space of truth and begin the journey of life beyond thought alone.

# Remember

Most of your thinking on a daily basis is absorbed by what the
created self needs and how it wants to feel

---

The created self does not like presence, or being without
thought, because without thought it cannot exist

---

To find the truth for yourself is first to understand the
transient and ever-changing nature of your thoughts

---

If you can witness your mental-emotional reactive patterns as
they happen, then that dimension is already emerging in you.

---

You can move into a space of truth and begin
the journey of life beyond thought alone

# Quote

---

"For every minute you are angry you lose sixty seconds of happiness."
-Ralph Waldo Emerson-

---

## Chapter Twenty-one:

## Finally Free

In this book, I have often referred to being happy and having real peace of mind, but what does that mean exactly? At the heart of that statement, humans just want to be free of themselves, and they want freedom from what is holding them back from being happy and having a peaceful life, which is the created self. However, here lies the paradox: losing themselves is also their biggest fear. As I realized many years into my life, what I wanted and feared were the same thing. I wanted freedom from the created self, yet I was afraid of losing the very thing I had invested all of my time into preserving and creating. When you have believed with conviction in the workings of your mind and are convinced it knows best, why would you ever question or want to be free of it? It is all you know about yourself, and you believe it is the part of you which creates the desire to be happy. You also think it is where the inspiration and motivation to live a great life comes from. Without the created self, how could you feel alive and experience life?

    The true essence of living with freedom is to experience life and not attach yourself to it. It means being connected to every moment of every day, to live with the awareness of who you are beyond this created version we call "me". Every experience is there to be appreciated and valued. To live a truly great life, you must detach yourself from your experiences and just feel them independently for what they offer. When you attach yourself to experience, you make it about the created self, and in return, every experience isn't perceived for what it brings and gives the already ever-greedy created self something else to cling onto. Can't you see the trouble this brings into your life? Once you attach yourself to an experience, you dilute the presence of being and don't enjoy it from its true source. You make it about yourself. It's no surprise you're so confused about who you are and about your life in general; the created mind's version is responsible for using all of the events in your life to keep you away from the truth and from its own annihilation. On recognizing the truth about who you are, everything you go through in your life will merely be another experience, however small or large your created self tries to make it. Experiences you go through have a much more profound lesson in them. Unfortunately, you cannot understand them while you are attached to them. Ask yourself this question: "If I am my experience, then who is the experiencer?" You cannot be both. Seeing this truth opens up a whole new world. You notice the experience for what it is and you now operate from a different level, one which has no limits. You may find moving from the created self difficult at first, but with a steadfast attitude and alert awareness, this process will happen automatically. The true self comes through eventually.

Every experience will be appreciated because of its deeper meaning to you. Even the experiences you don't enjoy will not affect you. Instead, you will accept them in that moment for what they bring and allow the experiences to pass. Knowing the truth will also allow you to let go of your past experiences that may still be affecting you. It is only the created self that doesn't want you to forget about the past because it is built up of the past and does not want you to release yourself from it. Without past and future experiences, the created self cannot survive.

Having freedom and being happy can be defined in many ways too. Some believe it's success and money that will ultimately free them from being unhappy. Others think it's the much-needed career break or promotion, the perfect life partner that seems to be eluding them, or better health that would make all the difference. During your lifetime, your definition and opinion of what you need to be happy and fulfilled continues to change, but whatever your missing piece is, it is safe to say it will never be enough until you attain a mindset that is conducive to knowing your true self first. It is imperative that you remain conscious that happiness is knowing the truth about who you are and not the means to an end for the created self. As I have alluded to previously, there is nothing wrong with wanting to be successful and trying to achieve more in your life. The only difference is that you must question the intent. What I mean by that is, who are you doing this for? If you are only trying to enhance the self-image of the created self, then the success you achieve will only at some point bring you more pain and misery.

The law of the created self has an opposite reaction to everything. Something perceived to be good now will one day bring you pain. When you know and operate away from the created self, everything you achieve and do has a much more inherent meaning to it and becomes easier to attain. Hence, it is imperative for your peace of mind and happiness that you look to your true self to claim back your life and be free from the chains of this insane belief about who you are. You are already what you are. You're pretending to be something else. Wake up and realize that if even after all this living, searching, striving, you're still not happy and free, then something needs to change.

The created self loves to rate everything and look for reasons why something isn't the way it should be, and that it deserves more. Nothing is ever enough for the self you have created with your mind. The only real purpose and thing of value to achieve in your life is to connect with your true self. Once you can reach a level of understanding, you now have something attainable, and that is permanent. You will always feel totally fulfilled in this space, knowing that you are not only discovering your true self but ending the very thing that is the problem. We all have a responsibility to find our true life's purpose. We owe it to ourselves. Nothing else will ever be of any value unless we begin to understand who we are. When we make a concerted effort to witness the workings of the created self, we stop acting on its negative beliefs that take us away from ever being fulfilled and at peace. We can now finally take our lives towards the freedom we all want and desire.

We all need to realize the true value of this amazing gift of life. It requires time and a focus on designing a great life. It takes courage and above all else wisdom to find and follow your true self. Once you've discovered your true self, you can begin to have a true sense of well-being and a feeling of complete freedom.

# Remember

---

You are not who you think you are.
You are so much more!

---